Access to Inner Worlds

The Story of Brad Absetz

COLIN WILSON

Rider

London Melbourne Sydney Auckland Johannesburg

Rider & Company

An imprint of the Hutchinson Publishing Group

17–21 Conway Street, London W 1 P 6 J D

Hutchinson Group (Australia) Pty Ltd
30–32 Cremorne Street, Richmond South, Victoria 3121
PO Box 151, Broadway, New South Wales 2007

Hutchinson Group (NZ) Ltd
32–34 View Road, P O Box 40–086, Glenfield, Auckland 10

Hutchinson Group (S A) Pty Ltd
P O Box 337, Bergvlei 2012, South Africa

First published 1983
© Colin Wilson 1983

Acknowledgement

For the extract from *The Permanent Goethe* by Thomas
Mann, Ed., copyright © 1948 by The Dial Press. Permission
granted by The Dial Press.

Set by Colset Pte Ltd, Singapore

Printed in Great Britain by The Anchor Press Ltd
and bound by Wm Brendon & Son Ltd,
both of Tiptree, Essex

British Library Cataloguing in Publication Data
Wilson, Colin
    Access to inner worlds.
    1. Self-discovery
    I. Title
    158'.1   BF697

ISBN 0 09 150080 X (cased)
ISBN 0 09 150081 8 (paper)

For Brad Absetz and
Jurij Moskvitin

Contents

1
Beyond Left-Brain Consciousness

On the afternoon of Sunday 3 January 1960, I was about to leave the house when the telephone rang. A man with a strong foreign accent explained to me that he was from some international press agency, and that he was ringing to tell me that Albert Camus had been killed in a car accident. For a moment I suspected a joke; my friend Bill Hopkins often rang me up pretending to be a Chinese laundry, or the head of the women's section of the KGB with just one vacancy for a male. The journalist soon convinced me that he was genuine; he knew too much about the accident to be making it up. Camus had been driving back to Paris with his friend Michel Gallimard when a front tyre burst. The car hit a tree and Camus was catapulted through the rear window; he was killed instantly.

On my way to the station a few minutes later – I was going to meet my wife – I tried to grasp the fact that Camus was dead. He worked for Gallimard, my French publisher, and had been about to write an introduction to my second book. I had met him in Paris and found him immensely likeable. Yet now, trying to focus the meaning of his death, I found myself unable to summon any reaction. It was like ringing a doorbell and hearing no sound. When I asked myself: 'How do you feel about his death?', the answer was a kind of: 'So what?'

Yet, in a sense, this was appropriate. The starting-point of all Camus's work is this sense of meaningless, that feeling of alienation that he called 'the absurd'. Meursault, the hero of *L'Etranger*, experiences this same inability to react to the

11

death of his mother. 'Mother died today. Or maybe yesterday; I can't be sure. . . .' He is not heartless or self-centred, merely *trapped* in the present. It would not even be true to say he is bored; he seems reasonably contented. But his sense of meaning is limited to what goes on at the end of his nose.

Then, at the end of the book – when he has been sentenced to death for killing an Arab – he experiences a surge of anger that brings insight. 'It was as if that great rush of anger had washed me clean, emptied me of hope, and . . . I laid my heart open to the benign indifference of the universe.' Staring at the stars he comments: 'To feel it so like myself . . . made me realize that I'd been happy, and that I was happy still.' This seems an odd statement from a man who seems to plod through life like a blinkered horse. Is it possible to be happy without knowing it?

Here we confront a paradox; for the answer is yes. We have all experienced the moments that William James calls 'melting moods', when it suddenly becomes perfectly obvious that life is infinitely fascinating. And the insight seems to apply *retrospectively*. Periods of my life that seemed confusing and dull at the time now seem complex and rather charming. It is almost as if some *other person* – a more powerful and mature individual – has taken over my brain. This 'higher self' views my problems and anxieties with kindly detachment, but entirely without pity. Looking at problems through his eyes, I can see I was a fool to worry about them.

If I could remain in this state all the time – or at least, summon it at will – life would be a continual adventure. And this is the maddening absurdity. For during these moments of intensity and affirmation, we can see that it would be *so easy* to maintain this insight. Whenever we face crisis or difficulty, we can see that life without it would be delightful. Raskolnikov in *Crime and Punishment* says that he would rather stand on a narrow ledge for ever than die at once. But we do not have to go that far to see that life without crisis or misery is full of potentiality. I can recognize this truth even when a minor inconvenience disappears. If the lavatory is out of order for a week, I heave a sigh of relief when the plumber finally appears. The fact that I can now stop flushing it down with buckets of water becomes an extension of my freedom, a source of active pleasure. And it continues to be so until I begin 'taking it for granted'. When this happens, I slip into the state in which Meursault spends most of his life: happy without realizing it.

What is wrong with human beings? Why is it, as Fichte says, that 'to be free is nothing; to *become* free is heavenly'? Why is it that we seem to be unable to appreciate our freedom unless it is under threat? Why do human beings seem to live in an almost permanent state of unreality?

The basic answer is that human beings are the only creatures who spend 99 per cent of their time living *inside their own heads*. Sherlock Holmes used to keep a cabinet filled with press cuttings on every subject under the sun, so that if he was confronted with a mystery involving, let us say, an American oil millionaire, he could send Watson to the file for a sketch of the man's career. We all have similar filing cabinets inside our own heads, and they contain 'press cuttings' (some of them rather brittle and faded) of everything that has ever happened to us. Confronted by some irritating problem, we can look in the file to see whether anything like it has ever happened in the past. This means that we can brood on these matters while lying in bed with our eyes closed; the experience is all there in the filing cabinet.

But this method has its disadvantages. When I am dealing with the real world, I react to it in a sensible and balanced manner, and find many problems exhilarating. When I am lying in bed with my eyes closed, I am out of touch with reality; the result is that I am likely to over-react to problems, and work myself into a state of anger or frustration or depression. And even when I am supposed to be 'in touch with reality' during the day, I spend a great deal of my time in that library with its filing cabinets. Every time I stare out of a window, or wait at a bus stop, or sit in the midst of a traffic jam, I descend into my mental world, and virtually lose touch with reality.

This ability to 'live inside our heads' is, of course, one of the greatest evolutionary advances made by the human race. Grey Walter remarks in his book on the brain that a chimpanzee 'cannot maintain a mental image long enough to reflect on it'.

Human beings can not only maintain mental images; they can spend hours at a time in a world of imagination. The purpose of this faculty is to enable us to envisage the future and anticipate its problems. Yet it has one enormous disadvantage. It means that we can, without even noticing it, lose contact with the world of actuality. There is an old joke of a man going to borrow a lawn-mower from his next door neighbour. On the way there, he imagines his neighbour saying: 'Why don't you buy one of your own?', to which he replies: 'Because I can't afford it.' 'Then why not get one on hire purchase?' 'I don't like being in debt.' 'Yet you're willing to come and borrow mine. . . .' At this point he meets his neighbour in the front garden and shouts: 'Keep your bloody lawn-mower. . . .' We all allow similar fantasies to undermine the sense of reality. And we are totally unaware of how far the fantasy has taken on a life of its own. Man is the only animal who is prone to insanity; and this is because he spends so much time in this suffocating prison inside his own head. His fantasies creep all over him, like ivy on a tree, until they drain away his life.

This is why the moments of reality – like Meursault's sense of relief and happiness – come as such a shock. Our mental apparatus reduces things to oversimplified images, and we come to accept these as a fair copy of the reality 'out there'. And then, in some moment of relaxation and happiness, the reality bursts through, infinitely more exciting than our dehydrated mental images. It is more real, heavier, richer, more beautiful, and it fills us with a desire to live for ever. Camus describes such a moment at the end of his story 'The Woman Taken in Adultery'. Her 'adultery' is with the African night, which enters into her being and possesses her. 'Not a breath, not a sound, except at intervals the muffled crackling of stones that the cold was reducing to sand. . . . After a moment, however, it seemed to her that the sky above her was moving in a sort of slow gyration. In the vast reaches of the dry, cold night, thousands of stars were constantly appearing, and their sparkling icicles, loosened at once, begin to slip gradually towards the horizon. Janine could not tear herself away from contemplating these drifting flares. She was turning with them. . . .' The passage brings to mind another 'woman taken in adultery' – Lawrence's Lady Chatterley – and her own mystical sense of living nature as she returns home after love-making: 'in the twilight the world seemed a dream; the trees in the park seemed bulging and surging at anchor on a tide, and the heave of the slope to the house was alive'. And Dostoevsky's Alyosha experiences a similar sensation as he looks at the stars: 'there seemed to be threads from all those innumerable worlds of God, linking his soul to them'; he flings himself, weeping, on his knees, to kiss the earth.

Yet all that has happened – to Janine, to Constance Chatterley, to Alyosha Karamazov – is that they have walked out of the prison inside their own heads, to confront the reality of the world. William Blake writes:

Five windows light the cavern'd Man: thro' one he breathes the air;
Thro' one hears music of the spheres; thro' one the eternal vine
Flourishes, that he may receive the grapes; thro' one can look
And see small portions of the eternal world that ever groweth;
Thro' one himself pass out what time he please; but he will not,
For stolen joys are sweet, & bread eaten in secret pleasant.

If the 'five windows' refer to the senses, then the passage is incomprehensible, since it implies that we can walk outside our senses, and we know this to be impossible. But what Blake actually means is that man lives in a cave inside his own head, *yet he does not have to*. He can 'pass out what time he please'. He can 'snap out' of the dream-like state, and reassert his sense of reality.

The comment about 'bread eaten in secret' is equally puzzling unless we recognize that Blake is speaking about the dream-like state in which we spend most of our time. Provided the daydreams are pleasant, the cave inside the head is a warm and comfortable place. The danger is in allowing ourselves to mistake it for the real world. Flaubert's *Madame Bovary* and Tolstoy's *Anna Karenina* are cautionary tales about women who make this mistake; both commit suicide. Tolstoy had enough insight to make Anna wake up as she is about to be killed by a train, and recognize that this is preposterous – that death is the last thing she wants.

But how is it possible that even the most habitual daydreamer could do anything as absurd as committing suicide? Children, of course, find it easy to sink into states of black depression – particularly imaginative children – because their knowledge of the world is so small that they habitually turn molehills into mountains. But surely the stupidest and most self-absorbed adult ought to know better? And the answer, once again, is that the astonishing pace of human evolution is to blame. More than any other animal, we have the power to focus upon particulars; we possess a kind of mental microscope which enables us to narrow down our attention to a single problem. A microscope can make a flea look as big as a horse. It can also turn a minor annoyance into a major catastrophe. Once we enter the state of adulthood, we spend so large a proportion of our lives dealing with problems that we forget their actual scale. We forget to take our eye away from the microscope. To use a slightly different analogy: it is as if we possessed a pair of reading glasses – for close-up work – and a pair of long-distance glasses. We get so used to wearing the reading glasses that we forget to remove them when we go out for a walk, and find ourselves peering short-sightedly at the scenery.

Then some crisis – or moment of delighted anticipation – reminds us that we ought to be wearing the long-distance glasses. And the moment we put them on, we experience a revelation. Everything becomes clear and real. All petty anxieties drop from our shoulders. We feel like laughing aloud. Suddenly, it becomes obvious that all the miseries and anxieties were a stupid mistake, due to the wrong glasses. There is a feeling of relaxation and happiness that seems to express itself in the words: 'Of *course!*'

But 'of course' what? If we could answer that question we would have solved one of the most basic problems of human development.

And the starting-point must be the 'glimpse of reality'. T. E. Lawrence describes a typical one in *Seven Pillars of Wisdom*: 'We started out on one of those clear dawns that wake up the senses with the sun, while the intellect, tired after the thinking of the night, was yet abed. For an hour or two, on such a morning, the sounds, scents, and colours of the world struck man individually and directly, not filtered through or made typical by thought: they seemed to exist sufficiently by themselves. . . .'

This is the sensation we experience after an illness, when we first begin to convalesce. The heart seems to be wide-open to experience, and, as Lawrence says, we no longer 'filter' it through our critical mechanism. It is the feeling we sometimes get on the first day of a holiday. Reality comes flooding in through the senses, and it has upon us the same effect as food on an empty stomach.

One of the most important discoveries of recent decades is the one for which Roger Sperry has received the Nobel Prize: the recognition that this 'critical mechanism' is located in the left side of the brain, while the mechanism that enables us to 'appreciate' reality is located in the right. Of the two cerebral hemispheres – the parts of the brain that press against the top of the skull – the left deals with language and reason, the right deals with feeling and intuition. (For some reason that is still not understood, the left brain controls the right side of the body, with all its muscles, and the right brain controls the left side.) Looked at from above, they look like the two halves of a walnut. Sperry discovered that if the 'bridge' between the two halves is severed – as it is in some cases to cure epilepsy – the patient turns into two different persons. One man tried to button up his flies with his right hand (connected to the 'rational' side of his brain) while the other hand undid them. Another patient tried to embrace his wife with one arm while the other pushed her away. A patient who had been given some wooden blocks to arrange into a pattern (a right-hemisphere activity) tried without success to do it with his right hand. His other hand kept trying to help, and the right kept impatiently knocking it away, as if to say: 'Let *me* do this.' Finally, he had to sit on his left hand to stop it from interfering.

Now in this case, it is obvious that the left hand ought to have been given its own way; for it is connected to the right brain, and could *see* the answer. But before we jump to the conclusion that the right is a hero and the left a villain, we should note that the right is also at the mercy of negative emotions. When one split-brain patient became angry with his wife, his left hand tried to hit her; the other hand defended her and held the left hand tightly.

The left brain, then, is the critic, the 'restrainer', the part of T.E. Lawrence that kept him from appreciating reality – except when he got up so early that the left brain was still asleep.

This enables us at least to begin to explain what that 'Of course!' means. 'You', the ego, live in your left brain. When we say that man is the only creature who spends 99 per cent of his time inside his own head, we mean, in fact, inside his left cerebral hemisphere. And in the basement of the left hemisphere is the library full of filing cabinets – the stuffy room that we mistake for reality. In *Heartbreak House*, Hector asks Shotover: 'How long dare you concentrate on a feeling without risking having it fixed in your consciousness all the rest of your life?', and Shotover answers an hour and a half. We all know what he means. Obsessions get stuck in our heads. We brood upon past experience like a cow chewing the cud, regurgitating it and chewing it yet again. Finally, the experience has become shrunken and tasteless, like an old piece of chewing gum. *And yet we still mistake it for the real thing.*

It is upon the basis of this dry, tasteless experience that we base our major decisions on life. If I am asked whether I would like to go to the theatre on Saturday night, I recall previous visits to the theatre, try to remember what they were like, and say yes or no on the basis of those faded memories. Worse still, confronted by some tiresome problem, I remember the last time I had to deal with a similar problem, and my energies drain away; I feel exhausted and depressed before I have even started. And this 'assessment' is made upon completely false data – a tasteless piece of chewing gum.

Yet we make this mistake habitually, all the way through our lives – *habitually undermining our own vitality.*

This is why that 'glimpse of reality' makes us say: 'Of course!' We have seen through the error – the mistake that has caused a constant leak of energy, that has stolen so much of our happiness, that has prevented us from achieving a fraction of what we might have achieved.

This brings another interesting recognition. For more than two thousand years, philosophers have been producing gloomy and negative assessments of human existence: Ecclesiastes says there is nothing new under the sun and that life is vanity; the Buddha says it is all illusion; Aristotle says it is better not to have been born. Very few philosophers seem to have much good to say about life. Because these men are great thinkers, we are inclined to take their word for it. Yet now we see that thinking has its own limitations: the limitations of the left brain. No doubt Ecclesiastes and Aristotle *thought* they were taking everything into account; but they had left out precisely 50 per cent of human existence. They were mistaking an old piece of chewing gum for the real thing.

It is true that many philosophers – particularly among the mystics – have warned us against the danger of mistaking thought for reality. And in the past century, writers as different as Walt Whitman, G. K. Chesterton, D. H. Lawrence, Aldous Huxley and Henry Miller have repeated the message. But there is usually something oddly unsatisfying about these disciples of instinct and intuition. They seem to offer a poor second best. D. H. Lawrence fulminated against 'head consciousness' and advised us to trust the solar plexus; but his work offers no clear advice on what to *do*. In a sense, he is as pessimistic as the 'thinking' philosophers; some of his stories seem to suggest that man would be better off if he was born as a horse or a fox. Walt Whitman envied the cows because they were uncomplaining. But what *we* want to understand is the secret potentialities of consciousness. Rejecting the left brain in favour of the right is obviously no solution. I do not feel that human beings have made a mistake in evolving left-brain consciousness. For all its problems and anxieties, I still prefer the condition of being human to being a cow. What we need to know is how to go *beyond* left-brain consciousness.

The right-brainers, like the left-brainers, have left something important out of account. What? We can see the answer if we think again of Meursault's experience of the 'benign indifference of the universe', of Janine's experience of the African night, of Alyosha Karamazov's desire to kiss the earth. This is not simply a glimpse of the *external* reality. It is an internal reality that has opened up. Hesse expresses it with beautiful clarity in *Steppenwolf*, another novel about a man who finds himself trapped and suffocated in left-brain consciousness. At the end of a frustrating day he goes to a tavern to eat and drink; the wine causes a sudden relaxation into right-brain consciousness:

'A refreshing laughter rose in me. . . . It soared aloft like a soap bubble . . . and then softly burst. . . . The golden trail was blazed, and I was reminded of the eternal, and of Mozart and the stars. For an hour I could breathe once more. . . .'

The laughter is the equivalent of the 'of course' feeling; we always want to laugh aloud when tension gives way to relaxation. But what is important here is the phrase '*reminded* of the eternal, and of Mozart and the stars'. There was nothing to stop him *thinking* about Mozart and the stars at any time of the day. But he is referring not to thinking, but to a feeling of the *reality* of Mozart and the stars. It is as if an inner trapdoor had opened, leading into an immense Aladdin's cave.

What, then, has happened? In effect, Steppenwolf has brought his right and· left hemispheres into alignment. He has relaxed *into* right-brain consciousness. Another important observation made by scientists examining the differences between right and left is that the left is obsessed by time; the right seems to have little sense of time. This seems reasonable, since logic and language have a lineal and serial structure – like a chain – while patterns spread out sideways, so to speak. The left brain tends to hurry forward, its eyes fixed on the future, while the right strolls along with its hands in its pockets, enjoying the scenery. They are like two trains running on parallel tracks, but at different speeds. If the right can be persuaded to move faster, by working it into a state of excitement (as, for example, with exciting music), then the two trains can run side by side, and the passengers can lean out of the windows and talk to one another. The same effect can be achieved if the left can be persuaded to move slower. This is what Steppenwolf has done as he relaxes with his glass of wine. Hence the sudden feeling of reality.

So one of the main functions of the right brain is to add a dimension of *reality* to our experience. The world as seen by left-brain consciousness is flat, two-dimensional, little more than a sketch. The business of the right brain is to add a third dimension. It is this recognition of reality that brings the feeling of relief, the sense that 'all is well'. As absurd as it sounds, we live most of our lives upon the assumption that reality is unreal – two dimensional. We feel that it is flat, boring, too easily known. But when the right brain begins to do its proper work, we recognize the absurdity of this assumption: that the world is infinitely richer and more meaningful than the left can grasp.

This provides us with our first major clue to the solution of this problem. Even if the left cannot *see* the world as full of potentiality, it can hold on to the moments of insight and refuse to let go of them. If I know that present difficulties will end in triumph, I am un-discourageable; I merely have to know it intellectually. And if I can 'know' that reality actually has a third dimension, I shall never fall into the mistake of complaining that there is nothing new under the sun and that life is futile.

This is a point of considerable importance. So much of the literature of the past century has been concerned with boredom and frustration. Artsybashev wrote a novel called *Breaking Point* about a dull Russian town in which practically everybody commits suicide. He was arguing, in effect, that when life is seen without illusions, the only courageous decision is to refuse to go on. We can see the absurdity of the mistake. His characters lack sense of purpose, so they have become trapped in left-brain consciousness, which dehydrates the world of meaning. They have forgotten the trapdoor that leads into inner worlds.

This tendency to become trapped in left-brain consciousness is perhaps the greatest single danger that threatens us as a species. Every year, thousands of people commit suicide because they believe 'that is all there is' – they think this two-dimensional world of our everyday experience is the only reality. All mental illness is caused by the same assumption, which can be compared with the assumption of savages that an eclipse of the sun could mean the end of the world. A savage who knew the real cause of an eclipse might still experience a certain irrational anxiety as the sun became dark; but his basic attitude to the experience would be relaxed and rational. And if human beings could grasp this insight about right-brain consciousness, mental illness would finally become as rare as leprosy.

As soon as we glimpse this possibility of a balanced left-and-right consciousness, we can see it as the beginning of a whole range of new developments in human consciousness. Consider, for example, what happens when I read a novel. To some extent, I enter the world of the novelist; yet because my left brain is doing most of the work, scanning and interpreting the words, my experience of that mental world is only superficial. I can recall certain books I read in childhood – Dickens's *A Christmas Carol* and *The Old Curiosity Shop*, the opening chapters of *The Count of Monte Cristo*, Conan Doyle's *Lost World* and the Sherlock Holmes stories, Rider Haggard's *She* and *Cleopatra* – which made me feel as if I had entered a state of trance; I was living in the world of the book rather than in the 'real' world. My mind supplied that fictional world with smells and colours and tastes. In short, my right brain did its proper work of adding a third dimension of reality to the book.

Neither is it a matter of becoming absorbed in certain characters and events in fiction. I have slipped into that same state of total absorption when reading Whitehead's *Science and the Modern World* and William James's *Varieties of Religious Experience*. The right brain can add this same element of reality to ideas.

So the 'filing cabinet' inside the head is only part of the story. When consulted by the left brain, the cabinet may appear to contain only sheets of paper. But when the right brain can be persuaded to play its part, these sheets can be transformed by some alchemy into a living reality.

This enables us to see precisely what is wrong with those writers who are prophets of instinct, like D.H.Lawrence and Henry Miller. They may appreciate literature, yet they feel that books are 'just words', a kind of game that should not be confused with reality. But when a book is transformed by the right brain, it becomes another kind of reality, with claims to equality with the 'real world'.

This is why the past two centuries or so have been some of the most exciting in human intellectual history. In 1719, a political pamphleteer named Daniel Defoe produced *Robinson Crusoe*, and seven years later, Jonathan Swift published *Gulliver's Travels*. Defoe meant *Crusoe* to be a piece of realistic journalism – it was based upon the true story of a shipwrecked mariner – and Swift intended *Gulliver* as political satire. In fact, both had created a kind of magic carpet that could carry the reader off into the realms of imagination. In 1740 came Samuel Richardson's *Pamela*, the first novel actually written as an exercise in pure invention (or 'escapism' as we might now say), which created a sensation all over Europe. Until this time, the favourite recreational reading of bored housewives had been volumes of sermons – for the sermon, with its anecdotes and exhortations, also provided a higher vantage point from which one's own life could be surveyed. But as a magic carpet, the novel was as superior to the sermon as a jet plane is to the old-fashioned airship. In a few decades, England became a nation of avid readers; the same thing happened all over the civilized world. Bored housewives had gained 'access to inner worlds'. Caught up in the sad destiny of Clarissa Harlowe or young Werther, they could transform mere words into a living reality by adding the weight of their own experience.

The experience altered the mind of civilized man. Defoe, Swift, Addison, Johnson, Montesquieu were of a generation of realists. They were succeeded by a generation of dreamers, who placed feeling and desire above convention and duty. And a curious thing happened. Man suddenly noticed that nature was beautiful. Earlier generations had regarded mountains as impressive but inconvenient. These new romantics saw in them a reflection of their own inner mountain landscape. Nature was exciting because it reflected man's new sense of his own potentialities:

> To horse! – way o'er hill and steep!
> Into the saddle blithe I sprung;

The eve was cradling earth to sleep,
And night upon the mountain hung.
With robes of mist around him set,
The oak like some huge giant stood,
While with its hundred eyes of jet
Peered darkness from the tangled wood.

This is the young Goethe, and it conveys the excitement of a young man setting out to ride to his mistress. Poets like Goethe, Schiller, Byron, Shelley, Pushkin, seemed to have glimpsed new possibilities of freedom for the human spirit.

Then why did disillusion set in? Partly for the same reason that early experiments in flying ended in crashes. The romantics were too inexperienced to know how to handle this sense of freedom. Many of them thought themselves free to seduce any number of young ladies with a good conscience, then found themselves in violent conflict with their sense of human decency. Others preferred to escape boredom with the use of drugs and alcohol. Overtaken by physical and emotional reactions, most of them concluded that the vision of freedom had been a delusion – in which case, human life is futile and tragic. With its unprecedentedly high rate of suicide and early death, the romantic experiment was finally accounted a failure.

Yet a new generation of romantics – Dostoevsky, Mann, Hesse, Shaw, Yeats – began to understand that freedom can only be achieved through self-discipline. Dostoevsky achieved his vision of freedom when he believed he was about to die in front of a firing squad, and became aware of something that earlier romantics had only glimpsed in flashes: *that the real trouble with human beings is that we habitually exaggerate our feelings.* A man who thinks he is about to be shot realizes with absolute certainty that most of the problems that have made him miserable are unutterably trivial; if he could only get a second chance, he could guarantee never to be unhappy for the rest of his life.

Experiences of this type always bring the same insight. We make the habitual assumption that we consist of a mind and a body. But there is another kind of body: the emotional body. For practical purposes, my feelings and emotions constitute a separate entity. And this is what makes life so difficult. The emotional body wastes an enormous amount of my time with its damned feelings. The sun goes behind a cloud and I feel gloomy. Somebody fails to reply when I ask a question, and I feel rejected. I trip over the pavement and feel accident-prone. I miss a bus and feel unlucky. I open my bank statement and feel apprehensive. I remember something I have forgotten to do and feel guilt-stricken. Nearly all these 'feelings' are negative. When the sun comes out from behind a cloud, I usually fail to notice it. When my bank statement shows a credit balance, I take it for granted. When I catch a bus, I am usually thinking about something else. So on the whole, the emotional body is a dreary bore, groaning at my failures and undervaluing my successes.

When some crisis awakens my sense of urgency, I suddenly realize how easy it would be to discipline the emotional body, and tell it to keep its stupid feelings to itself. How? That question can be answered by anyone who casts his mind back to such a situation. A real emergency has the effect of 'stiffening the sinews', arousing 'vital reserves'. Minor anxieties are instantly suppressed with a mental gesture that is rather like compressing a spring. With that threatening gesture, they instantly subside, like a whining child who realizes he has gone too far and that the heavy hand is about to descend.

This explains one of the minor mysteries of human psychology: why we go out of our way to look for challenges. Why should anybody want to become a Member of Parliament or the chairman of a sub-committee? Why, for that matter, should anyone want to climb a mountain? The old explanation, 'because it's there', is no answer. But every challenge arouses in us the kind of vital energy necessary for bullying the emotional body into silence. It sits on our shoulders, like the Old Man of the Sea with his legs wrapped around Sinbad's neck, slowly choking us to death – until an emergency arises. Then, with a single jerk, we throw him off. And suddenly, we can breathe again. Unfortunately, we do not follow Sinbad's lead, and beat out his brains while he lies on the ground. We forget him, and allow him to sneak back as soon as our thoughts are elsewhere. . . .

The first thing we observe when the Old Man has been

unseated is that life becomes far richer and more exciting. The Old Man's task, apparently, is to try to make us tired of life by keeping us entangled in triviality. He keeps on reacting to every minor problem as if it was the end of the world, and finally he convinces us that life is one long series of dreary obstacles. My only real ally against him is my reason, my ability to tell myself: 'Don't be stupid – this is not important.' If the Old Man can persuade someone to commit suicide, he has scored a real triumph.

Conversely, a man who had achieved what the Buddha called 'enlightenment' – permanent freedom from the Old Man – would live in an unwavering state of serene intensity. In this state, the external world is seen to be endlessly fascinating because, like a mirror, it reflects the immense depths of the internal world.

The past two centuries have been one of the most important periods in human history. For the first time, large numbers of human beings have been freed from the pressing involvement with physical reality. They have learned that it is not simply entanglement in mere physical process. Life lived under these conditions is basically futile and repetitive. We begin to live only when we learn to descend into ourselves as a coal miner is transported deep into the earth.

But *how*? How do we begin to go about making the descent?

The story I now propose to tell is of a man who stumbled accidentally on the 'trick', and whose life has been totally transformed by it.

2
Ten Days in Viittakivi

Some time in 1980, a Finnish correspondent, Matti Veijola, wrote to ask me whether I would be interested in attending a seminar in Finland for ten days in the summer of 1981. I had only once been to Finland – in 1960, on my way to Leningrad, and I had been impressed by my glimpses of its lakes and pine forests. For me, Finland meant the symphonies of Sibelius and the songs of Kilpinen, and that extraordinary novel by Alexis Kivi called *Seven Brothers*. The idea of an extended visit sounded pleasant, particularly since I could take my family.

In fact, the holiday – in the August of 1981 – came at exactly the right time. I had just completed the hardest four months work of my whole life. I had been commissioned to write a book on the poltergeist, with a delivery date of 30 June; and by the end of January I had finished the basic research and was ready to start typing. At this point, another publisher asked me if I would like to provide the text of an illustrated book on witch-craft, a subject I already knew reasonably well. Then *Reader's Digest* asked me if I could write them a short novel about Rasputin, of whom I had once written a biographical study. The terms were tempting, and since writers are habitually short of cash, I accepted both offers, assuming that the publisher of *Poltergeist* would allow me a couple of extra months for delivery of the typescript. I was mistaken. They had scheduled the book for autumn publication; an editor was waiting to get to work on it the moment it arrived, and to rush it to the printer. So it looked as if I had to write three books in four months. The prospect made my heart sink. The book on witchcraft would not be too difficult, since the text had to be written in sections – which meant there were no problems of construction. But a novel may simply refuse to go in the right direction, and have to be started again from the beginning. (For twenty-five years now I have been writing a novel called *Lulu*, and must have started it a hundred times.) Yet I couldn't afford to discard a single day's writing. The same was true of the poltergeist book; 120,000 words in eight weeks meant 15,000 words a week, or ten pages every single day, with no time for revision. Moreover, poltergeists are singularly repetitive creatures, behaving like disembodied football hooligans; I was not sure how I was going to spin out their boringly predictable activities for 120,000 words – this was a hurdle I would have to take when I came to it.

The very thought of all that non-stop typing, without time for relaxation, made me feel trapped. In 1973, I had been under similar pressure, and had begun to experience 'panic attacks' – bouts of sudden fear and intense depression. I had struggled my way out of these with common sense and a certain amount of self-analysis. Now the old sensations of unease began to return – a feeling I call 'the burning-rubber smell' – as if the brakes are beginning to smoulder. On the morning when I received the letter saying *Poltergeist* had to be delivered on time, I had been to see my doctor; he told me I was suffering from high blood pressure and had to lose two stone in weight. He also arranged an appointment with a specialist about a problem of internal bleeding that sounded ominously like cancer. When I got back from the doctor, I went to my desk to write about the burning and torture of the Bamberg witches; as I wrote I began to experience a 'sinking' sensation, accompanied by the old feeling of panic. In such moments, it suddenly seems that the floor of our sanity is very frail, and might collapse like thin ice. There is a feeling of energy draining away, and a suspicion that life is a battle that has been lost in advance. I forced myself to go and look for a reference book that I needed – although the action seemed meaningless – and stood in front of the bookcase, struggling with the sinking sensation. It was like trying not to be sick. Then I went back to my typewriter, gritted my teeth against the sense of misery and futility, and went on writing. At some point, I had to lean forward to pick up something I had dropped on the floor. Quite suddenly, the oppression vanished – as abruptly as the sun coming out from behind a cloud. With an almost dizzy feeling of astonishment and triumph, I realized that my emotions had been 'trying it on', having a tantrum, and that they had suddenly decided to give up. And at once I saw with great clarity that human beings possess *two bodies*. One is the physical body, the other – just as real, just as self-contained – is the emotional body. Like the physical body, the emotional body reaches a certain level of growth, and then stops. But it stops rather sooner than the physical body. So most of us possess the emotional body of a retarded adolescent. And as soon as we find ourselves under pressure, as soon as life begins to look difficult, the emotional body bursts into tears and tries to run away.

That insight was a turning-point. But since I had four months of non-stop writing ahead of me, and the anxieties about my physical condition, that was not the end of the matter. I lay awake for hours at night, trying to stop the pounding of my heart, and to resist thoughts that dragged me into depression. I knew that my salvation lay in that thread of pure will, the determination not to give way; yet there was always a fear that the thread might eventually snap under the strain. I finished the 50,000 words on witchcraft in just over a month, and felt a certain irritation when the publisher told me that he had over-estimated the space available and would have to cut out 10,000 words – a whole week's work. I settled down to the Rasputin novel, which fortunately went well for the first hundred pages, although there were days when I felt so low that I could eat only the occasional digestive biscuit. Halfway through, it was clear that I wasn't going to succeed in compressing his life into 60,000 words – I had already done 40,000, and hadn't even got him as far as St Petersburg. . . . Eventually I finished it on time, 15,000 words too long – leaving *Reader's Digest* the problem of cutting – and on the day after I typed the last paragraph, began *Poltergeist*. Again, the gods were with me. New information, new ideas, turned up at exactly the right moment. I was well behind schedule, but the publisher told me that if I could deliver most of the book by the agreed date, I could have another fortnight to write the final chapter. I began to experience a sort of grim exhilaration as I forced myself into the final gallop. I finished the book with several days to spare, and then went on to write six articles for a magazine of which I am advisory editor. At the end of the four months, I had the satisfaction of calculating that I had written a quarter of a million words, the length of Joyce's *Ulysses*.

A week later we set out for Finland – Joy, myself, and our two boys Damon and Rowan. At last I had time to take stock. My most powerful ally in the previous four months had been my power of reason. My emotions had staged a full-scale revolt, trying to convince me that if I pressed on at this pace, the result would be nervous breakdown. My body, on the whole, had behaved rather better, in spite of the high blood pressure and the blood in my urine that made me suspect cancer (it turned out to be nothing worse than a broken vein). What was most important was a recognition – to which I shall return in the last chapter – that if I could drag myself out of a state of fatigue and depression into 'normality', then there was no reason why I should not drag myself out of normality into a state of far higher energy and intensity. We have, in fact, far greater control over our inner being than we realize. The answer lay in developing a certain power of realism, of objectivity. When we experience moods of fatigue or depression, it only takes some real crisis or danger to show us that the depression was sheer self-indulgence. If we could simply hold fast to this vision – which reason tells us to be true – we would never again be victimized by our emotions.

But the hard truth is that this control can only be achieved by confronting the emotions head-on and bullying them into submission. In the *Seven Pillars*, Lawrence describes how, after a halt in the desert, they realized that one of their number was missing. Lawrence turned his camel and went back to search. But the camel disliked leaving the main group, and kept trying to turn back; Lawrence had to force it to go on. Throughout the first half of 1981, my emotions had behaved like Lawrence's camel every time I sat down at my typewriter. And I now had the satisfaction of having taught the camel a degree of obedience.

We drove to London airport on the day Prince Charles was married, and the radio babbled endlessly about the ecstatic crowds; it was impossible to find out what was happening elsewhere in the world. At the Post House Hotel they even offered us a slice of wedding cake, to the surprise of our smallest boy, who speculated that it must have been enormous. The following day we flew to Helsinki.

The bearded man who met us at the barrier had a slight American accent and a quiet manner; he introduced himself as Brad Absetz, one of the teachers at Viittakivi. When I asked where he'd parked the car, he explained that Viittakivi didn't have a car - so we had a four-stage journey ahead of us: by bus into Helsinki, by train to Hämeenlinna, by bus to Hauho, then by taxi to Viittakivi. It is a measure of how far I had succeeded in controlling my sense of boredom that I accepted all this without an inward groan.

In Helsinki, with an hour to wait for the train, we went to a tea shop. It was a curiously old-fashioned place - a small room that looked liked a Victorian parlour, with a bird cage hanging from the wall; on a table in the centre of the room stood a huge cake-stand with all kinds of sticky pastries; we helped ourselves and took our tea over to the curtained window. I could imagine that this place had looked exactly the same at the time of Ibsen and Strindberg. While we drank tea, Brad told us more about the Viittakivi centre. It sounded not unlike the Esalen Institute near San Francisco, except that at Viittakivi the subjects ranged from world religions to organic farming. It had been founded by American Quakers after the war, in association with the Finnish Settlement Federation; this explained how an American like Brad had come to be involved.

On that first meeting, Brad did not strike me as in any way unusual - certainly not the kind of person about whom I might want to write a book. I found him relaxed and easy to talk to, and in some subtle way definitely not the type of American that I had met at Esalen - serious-minded students of Zen and Group

Therapy. But he was not the kind of person you would notice in a crowd. The main thing that struck me about him was that he seemed to be at ease and at peace, like a man sitting in front of his own fireside. He made me think of that earlier generation of Americans, like Henry James and Henry Adams, who had come to Europe looking for a sense of the historical past. If that was what Brad was looking for, he seemed to have found it.

The train pulled out of the station, past the harbour, and we were soon in the open countryside. There is something very soothing in the green, flat Finnish landscape, with its wooden houses and glimpses of water between the trees. As we sat in the restaurant car, drinking watery beer, I experienced suddenly that curious sense of satisfaction that can only be described in the words 'being where you are'. That sounds absurd only until we reflect that for most of our lives we are *not* where we are. I am walking down a lane in Cornwall, but only my body is there; my mind is 'elsewhere.' It is not in any particular place; it is just 'not all there' – a phrase we also use for the mentally defective. And then, beyond a certain point of relaxation, it happens. The left brain slows down; suddenly, it is walking in step with the right. And you are there, in the present moment, wholly and completely. You can taste the flavour of your own consciousness.

Casually, I asked Brad whether he had ever done any writing – the kind of polite question you ask a travelling companion on a long journey. He said: 'I once wrote some poems' – the kind of answer you expect from a travelling companion you know to be literate. Then, after a pause, he added: 'If you could say I wrote them.'

Oddly enough, I knew immediately what he meant. 'Who did, then?'

'I suppose you could say they wrote themselves.'

I said: 'The right brain?'

Brad looked at me curiously; but it was no time to open a conversation on split-brain physiology, with the children asking what was the Finnish for 'potato crisps'. And, unlike most poets, Brad did not seem anxious to pursue the subject. I said: 'I'd be interested to see them some time,' and we talked of other things.

Viittakivi stands in the midst of thick woodland, at the end of a lake that stretches for many miles. (In Finland there are so many interconnected lakes that it is possible to row for days.) Although it was late July, there was already a tang of autumn in the air – winter comes early that far north. The leaves were turning gold, and through the still air, you could hear a dog barking several miles away. The only drawback in this paradise is the mosquitoes – but Brad assured me they were scarce this year. (They seem to have the same power as vampire bats, of being able to feed unnoticed on their host – I watched one of them settle on the neck of Jormma (Brad's teacher-colleague) and make a three-course meal while he talked on unaware.)

Our chalet was comfortable, with a balcony that overlooked the lake. After some initial confusion – the taxi driver had absent-mindedly gone off with a case containing the children's pyjamas – we settled down to a cold supper. The only obvious drawback to the place was that it was 'dry'; alcohol was not actually forbidden; but there was none available on the premises, and the nearest state liquor store that sold wine was twenty miles away. I thought longingly about the magnums of Beaujolais I had seen at Heathrow, and had decided against buying because of the weight. . . . When we finally retired to bed, I lay awake for hours, made uneasy by the total stillness.

Breakfast was at eight; but since this was six o'clock London time, we decided to sleep late and make do with coffee and biscuits. The day was soft and grey. Since the first seminar was not being held until the afternoon, we caught the bus into Hauho, the nearest village, which is about five miles away. It is little more than a few shops, supermarkets and houses scattered around a cross-roads; unlike English villages, Finnish hamlets are mostly as nondescript as filling stations. In fact, most of Finland has an impressive air of order and neatness, as if run by an army of hard-working housewives. This intimidating air of efficiency is softened by the green, empty landscape, and the low volume of traffic on the roads; the country still seems to belong to the trees and birds. We bought groceries and cans of beer, went and looked at the church, and found a taxi that got us back in time for lunch. All meals in Viittakivi are self-service, and proved to be excellent. I grew particularly fond of a hard rye biscuit,

as brittle as a sheet of ice, and of a kind of peanut butter better than
any I have had in England or America.

Now it was time for work. While my family went boating on
the lake, I attended the opening seminar, which took place in the
large hall above the dining-room. It was a pleasant place, with
huge windows looking out over the lake and forest. There were
forty or fifty students, ranging in age from mid-teens to mid-
seventies. And, apart from regular lectures involving all the
students, there would be five study groups under particular
individuals, one being myself.

Brad opened the proceedings with a short speech about the
importance of being together and getting to know one another.
From anyone else it would have sounded trite; but Brad had a
quiet air of meaning every word he said. He felt we were there to
try to reduce the distance between individuals, to try to become a
kind of family. After this, every student introduced himself and
explained why he had come to Viittakivi – about half of them
spoke in Finnish and had to be translated. I was startled when one
of them, dressed in a kind of multi-coloured suit, went and sat
under the table and buried his face in his hands, peeping out at
intervals and shuddering nervously; after which he stood on the
table and performed a series of balletic poses. It looked as if he was
trying to communicate, like the man in G. K. Chesterton who
keeps hopping around on one leg; then I gathered that he was one
of the group-leaders, an actor who was here to teach us how to get
rid of our inhibitions through physical movement. . . .

I am not, I have to confess, the kind of person who enjoys
group activities. My brain tends to switch off, like a bored schoolboy in a class. In the wrong mood, I would have found all this
exasperating. But the past six months had made me very aware
that boredom is more to do with the person who is bored rather
than of the person who is doing the boring. We are too mechanical, and allow certain stimuli to *hypnotize* us into passivity. So I
deliberately refused to let my attention wander, and found that I
was becoming increasingly interested in these people and their
motives. It is true that I had seen it all before, in similar work-
groups in England and America: all the serious-minded people
who feel that civilization is too impersonal, that capitalism is

shameful, and that all governments are rather wicked. In fact, we had a number of extreme leftists and trade unionists among us, and they seemed to take it for granted that we all agreed that the rich must somehow be forced to surrender their ill-gotten gains. Yet there was an air of good humour about their idealism that made me feel they would not be too offended if I admitted that I regard socialists as well-meaning but muddle-headed brigands.

After an interminable amount of discussion – everybody wanted to talk – we finally worked out separate 'themes' for the work groups: creativity, society and responsibility (most of the leftists joined that one), self-expression through movement, and so on. My own group was concerned with the theme of inner freedom.

The following morning, I lectured to the whole student body for ninety minutes, and this was followed by two hours of discussion. Their stamina seemed to be tremendous. I was reminded of that story told by Berdyaev, of how a group in St Petersburg had stayed up until four o'clock one morning discussing the universe; when someone suggested it was time to go to bed, someone else said: 'No, we can't go to bed yet – we haven't decided whether God exists.' Our discussion was mainly political. I had finally decided I should nail my political colours to the mast rather than try to avoid discord; so I began by explaining how I had ceased to be a socialist after I wrote a book about Bernard Shaw which defended the socialist position. (When I re-read my own book in print, I saw that the arguments for socialism were nonsense.) I went on to speak about the animal need for territory, and pointed out that Proudhon was unaware of this fundamental urge when he formulated the principle that property is theft. To my surprise, a large number of people nodded enthusiastically – evidently I had been mistaken to suppose they were all leftists. The trade unionists, to do them justice, listened politely, but evidently felt that I had failed to understand their ideal of human brotherhood. And in the afternoon, I listened with equal politeness while three young leftists made stirring speeches about all the things that are obviously wrong with society, and how easy it would be to put them right if only people would refuse to

obey authority. Again, most of the audience nodded enthusiastically, and I concluded that they had an unusual capacity for
empathy.

Yet even my total disagreement with these ideas began to seem
fruitful. The stresses of the past months had taught me not to
'give way' to feelings of impatience and boredom. It was interesting to find that I could listen to ideas that struck me as naive
with detachment, even with sympathy. They simply made me
more aware that the basic hunger of human beings is for a certain
inner freedom. Leftists make the assumption that it can be
achieved through political reform, rather as a sexually inexperienced person imagines that losing your virginity completely
transforms your life. And the clear recognition that they were
mistaken made me aware of the precise nature of this inner freedom. I tried to explain it the following morning, in the first
session of our work group. There were seven or eight of us,
including Jormma, who had come along to translate. Most of the
group spoke English (indeed, two were Americans), but one lady
spoke only Finnish and Swedish. I found the prospect of non-stop
translation discouraging, but it proved to have its advantages. It
meant that I had to speak slowly, clearly and precisely, and that
everyone had a chance to reconsider it as it was translated.

I began by explaining Husserl's recognition that all perception
is 'intentional', that when we see something, we have to reach
out and grasp it, just like picking up an object in the hand. But this
act of 'grasping' has become unconscious – or rather, subconscious, hovering in the twilight between conscious and unconscious. From childhood on, we imagine that happiness is due to
circumstances – holidays, Christmas, unexpected pleasures, and
so on. In fact, the holiday only stimulates perception, so you
'grasp' twice as hard as usual. The result is that feeling of reality,
intensity. If we could deliberately re-programme the unconscious
mind to make twice as much effort, we could achieve intensity at
will.

As I write these words, they seem to me to say exactly what I
mean, and to express one of the most important truths human
beings are capable of grasping. But most of the group were only
able to half-grasp my meaning. I felt the irritating sense of non-

communication that I often feel after lecturing. That night, I lay awake for hours wondering how I could overcome their mistrust of the words – make them see straight to the reality behind the words. They wanted to 'do', not listen. And so the next day, I taught them a basic 'trick' for inducing deeper intentionality, the 'pen trick'.

Sudden crises cause the mind to 'contract', and when the danger vanishes, we expand with a feeling of relief. Graham Greene produced this effect by playing Russian roulette with his brother's revolver – pointing the loaded gun at his head, spinning the chambers and pulling the trigger. When there was just a click, he felt immense relief. 'It was as if a light had been turned on . . . and I felt that life contained an infinite number of possibilities.' This demonstrates the basic principle: that if the senses can contract violently, and then relax and expand, the result is a sense of relief, and a perception of the objective value of being alive.

Russian roulette is a dangerous way of causing this 'contraction'. It can be accomplished with less risk. One simple method is to take a pen or pencil, and hold it up against a blank wall or ceiling. Now concentrate on the pen as if it is the most important thing in the world. Then allow your senses to relax, so you see the pen against the background of the wall. Concentrate again. Relax again. Keep on doing this until you become aware of the ability to focus the attention at will. You will find that this unaccustomed activity of the will is tiring; it produces a sense of strain behind the eyes. My own experience is that if you persist, in spite of the strain, the result is acute discomfort, followed by a sudden immense relief – the 'peak experience'. The result is less spectacular – because less dangerous – than Greene's Russian roulette, but it is, in some ways, more interesting, for we become aware that we can alter our perceptions with an act of will. They are not just something that 'happens to us'.

Having explained this, and watched them practising the 'pen trick' for ten minutes or so, I was reminded of another exercise for the focusing of perception: Wilhelm Reich's breathing exercise. Reich made his patients lie on the floor, and take a deep breath; then they had to exhale slowly, allowing the out-going relaxation to move from the lungs, to the stomach, then down to the genitals. They had to repeat, as they did this: 'Out, down, through.' I had described the exercise in my book on Reich, and occasionally practised it when I wanted to relax; but I had never regarded it as particularly important, as Reich did. Now, on impulse, I asked my group to lie down on the floor, and accustom themselves to 'Reichian breathing' for five minutes or so. Then, at the end of that time, I asked them to raise their pens, stare at them, and combine the Reichian breathing with the 'pen trick'. I did this with them, and immediately understood that I had stumbled upon an interesting discovery. The breathing exercise induces deep relaxation and a sense of physical well-being. The pen exercise induces a sense of concentration and control. The two should, in theory, counteract one another's effect. But this does not happen. The control itself somehow becomes relaxed and confident, like a baby's breathing. After a few moments, I noticed the curious sense of exaltation, followed by a sensation as if floating out of my body. I glanced sideways at the others; all were lying there contentedly, obviously experiencing the same floating sensation. When the strain of holding up the pen became too great, we rested the arm, then started again. Time became unimportant; when I looked at my watch I could hardly believe that we had been lying there for more than half an hour, and that no one showed the slightest inclination to get up.

I had, in fact, accidentally come across a method of 'doing' as well as 'knowing'. For the remainder of our seminars it proved invaluable.

On most days, there were lectures as well as work groups. I attended many of these – on farming, education, community work, the problems of the Third World – although I seldom joined in the discussions afterwards. The truth is that I found some of the basic assumptions so naive that they were not worth the waste of breath. One pleasant, serious lady who had worked in Africa told us that she had become disillusioned with Finnish education because backward students lost heart when they failed to receive prizes, and so became the 'losers in society'. She looked forward to the day when there would be no more prizes – not only in schools, but in society. Competition, she said, was wicked and ought to be abolished. I tried to envisage a world in which all competition has been forbidden, and conjured up an image of a city of identical houses, with everyone dressed in grey uniforms. So I ceased to listen, and stared out of the window at the trees, which were distorted by the rain on the window panes. All I had to do was to imagine that I had just stumbled in out of a snow-storm, and was now relaxing in this pleasant, warm room. In moments like these, I could see the basic problem of human exis-tence with great clarity. We *need* stimulus to get the best out of us. When no stimulus is available, we settle dully into the present like a boat grounded by the tide. Yet in every crisis, we can see that these 'dull' situations should not be regarded as a misery, but as havens of peace. We should be able to use the imagination to recall situations of crisis, to generate instantly the power and drive that will lift us out of boredom like a rocket leaving the launching pad.

Later the same afternoon, I returned from a long walk in the woods to find a green plastic-covered notebook on my bed. Its title-page made it clear that these were some of the poems Brad had mentioned; he called them 'concentrates'. I opened the book casually in the middle without any particular interest – for the past twenty-five years I have received at least one unsolicited book of manuscript poems every week or two. But the first poem I read struck me as pleasingly epigrammatic:

> The world is full of promise
> when I am empty of threat.
> When the world is empty of threat
> I am full of the world.

I had been expressing the same idea to our work group that morning: that our innate mistrust of the world keeps us from grasping its possibilities, and that when this mistrust evaporates, because of some sudden relief, the world rushes into our senses like air into a vacuum. Brad had said the same thing with more concentration. I turned the page and read:

> Sadness is within me
> like a creeping gray mist
> blurring the landscape
> within me,
> like clinging blue smoke

rising from the fissures
within me,
like a melancholy melody
echoing through empty chambers
within me. . . .

The romantic melancholy was like the autumn landscape out-side, with grey clouds reflected in the lake. I poured myself a glass of wine and went on reading. His style had a pleasing simplicity:

The morning tide is out,
the beach washed clean and smooth
of even the sharply etched stepping of early birds;
the far water line
is undulating ever so slowly:
perfectly reflecting an inner seascape.

A lone gull
perches motionless and one-legged
on the single log-post
that breaks the gray, still surface of the morning
    sea,
and stares with unblinking calm
through the vanishing mists
towards an outer infinity.

What impressed me was that he seldom made the mistake of trying to be literary, or deliberately striking. I have never enjoyed Dylan Thomas because he seems to be trying too hard. Brad's 'concentrates' seemed effortless and sure-footed. They avoided sentimentality as easily as cleverness and display. Yet he could write lines as arresting as:

The dark orchids of deadly violence
Exude a warm fragrance of sweet bloodshed.

Just as a painter like Utrillo is able to capture a music of nostal-gia when he paints an empty street, so Brad seemed to be able to convey the essence of his experience in the barest and plainest of descriptions.

But the poem that impressed me most was the longest of all – one that began: 'Following the afterimage of a wise old man within me . . .'. (I quote it in full in the next chapter). Here the sense of describing an inner landscape is so strong that the poem must have sprung out of an almost hallucinatory experience. In his autobiography Jung described how, in a period of great stress after his break with Freud, he developed the curious ability to descend into his own mind, and to enter an apparently real landscape with real people – he called it 'active imagination'. In one of these strange waking dreams, Jung had also encountered a 'wise old man' named Philemon, and he records his conviction that in his conversations, 'he said things which I had not consciously thought. For I observed clearly that it was he who spoke, not I.' And this convinced Jung that 'there are things in the psyche which I do not produce'. There is in ritual magic a technique for entering the 'astral realms' which seems identical with Jung's 'active imagination', and Yeats has described briefly his own experiences with the method. Ouspensky also seems to have developed a similar ability, which he describes in *A New Model of the Universe.* But Brad was the first person I actually met who seemed to have developed the same ability.

A couple of hours later I met Brad in the sauna, and told him how exciting I found the poems. We sat together on the top step – which is the hottest part – until one of the children made it uninhabitable by ladling more cold water on to the hot coals, so that the heat became suffocating. So we went out and jumped into the lake, swam for a few minutes, then went back and repeated the process. After half an hour or so of this, we agreed we were sufficiently dehydrated, and I asked Brad if he felt like coming back for a glass of wine (an excellent Finnish-bottled Beaujolais that I had found in the state liquor store in Tampere). So we walked back over the low wooden bridge to my chalet, filled two tumblers to the brim, and clinked glasses. And when Brad began to tell me the story of how he came to write the 'concentrates' – and also to paint pictures and create metal sculptures – I encouraged him to begin at the beginning. It was a story so remarkable that I interrupted him to tell him he ought to write a book about it. He shrugged and said he didn't feel he was a writer. And as he talked on, the conviction came upon me that if he wouldn't write the book, then I would do it for him. Before he had finished, I even knew what I intended to call it: *Access to Inner Worlds*.

3

How to Contact the 'Other Self'

Early in 1961, Brad and his wife decided to adopt a newly-born baby, whose mother had been unable to take care of him. Like all adoptive parents, they wanted the opportunity to give love and protection to a child in need. But fate seemed to be against the venture from the beginning. During the early months of his life, the child had been left alone for long periods. This is, of course, the most vital formative period of a baby's life – the period at which 'imprinting' occurs. Konrad Lorenz made the observation that baby monkeys that do not receive the love of a mother during this period become incapable of forming emotional attachments; it seems that the give-and-take of love is imprinted within the first weeks of a child's life. And the baby had been left lying on one side for such long periods that one side of the head had become slightly flattened and malformed. From the beginning, their adopted child was 'difficult', screaming incessantly for attention, yet hardly seeming to respond to their attempts to give love.

In one sense at least, the child was fortunate; Brad and his wife were determined to do their best. With less responsible parents, the end result might have been a battered baby. It was not as if their son was an only child – they had three others, and a fourth arrived subsequently.

Then, when the boy was four and a half, he was found to have an abdominal cancer. The growth was removed, and the operation seemed to be successful. But a year later, a check-up revealed nodes of cancer scattered all over his internal organs. It was clear that the child was going to die. They decided to devote themselves to trying to make the last months of his life as complete and as rewarding as possible. The child seemed to grow up and change quite suddenly, as if in some way trying to make up for the years that were lost. He required constant attention; Brad and his wife took turns sitting up with him at night. The months extended to a year, then eighteen months. His eventual death was a shattering experience for everyone.

Brad's wife took it very badly. She was physically and emotionally exhausted, and delayed shock induced severe depression. Brad watched her descend into a subjective world of guilt and self-questioning; she lost interest in the outside world. Plunged into destructive self-analysis, she felt at times that she was damned, and that the whole world was damned with her. The depressions were balanced by a manic counter-phase in which she seemed to experience ecstasies of indescribable absolute freedom.

For hours at a time she lay on the bed, her eyes closed, struggling with guilt and depression. When she emerged from these inner spaces, that seemed to be as depressing as Piranesi's dungeons, Brad was always there beside her, ready to provide her with a link to the world of reality. At first, he was convinced that this was a growth-process, from which she would emerge stronger than ever. But gradually, it became clear that she was not improving. These descents into the mind can inaugurate a process of negative feedback, a kind of inner landslide of pessimism. When it became clear that her experiences were becoming frightful and unmanageable, Brad decided to look for outside help. A point came where, for the sake of the children, he felt it necessary to commit her to hospital. On the day a friend drove them there, he felt that he had reached a limit of physical and psychological exhaustion – that if something had complicated or prolonged the problems, he would have experienced physical and nervous collapse. After returning from the hospital, he slept for almost twenty hours.

But the ordeal was by no means over. For the next few years, the pattern of breakdown, hospitalization and partial recovery continued, and much of the responsibility for bringing up the children fell on Brad. During the day, he worked as a school-teacher. In the evening, he had to cope with his wife's illness, which now involved hallucinatory experiences. He would lie beside her for hours, waiting for her to emerge into reality. He learned to become relaxed, sensitively alert, inwardly poised for the moment when she would 'surface' and he could be of help. It was a continuation of the experience of the last years of their son's life.

It was in this state that he began to experience a curious sense of inner freedom, of release from the body. What happened then can be told in his own words:

'One day I was lying on my back on the bed beside my wife during one of these long periods of relaxed but concentrated sensitivity, when I noticed a clear but puzzling impulse in the muscles of my upper right arm, near the shoulder. What was clear about it was that the impulse was a movement impulse, i.e. the muscle was indicating a readiness to move. What was puzzling was that I had no thought or intention of moving my arm for any reason at the moment. However, being deeply relaxed, and having the underlying feeling of well-being that accompanied it, I was not alarmed, but I was rather curious, and I thought something like: "Well, if that arm wants to move, it may." It waited for a moment, during which the impulse got stronger, and my arm really did rise slowly from the bed and stop in mid-air as the movement impulse ceased. "This is really interesting," I thought. "What now?" After a brief moment I felt another clear impulse to move in that arm. Again I let it happen, and observed it with interest as my arm moved still further. For the next few minutes I allowed such impulses to move my arm (and soon it was both arms) through a series of movements. My attention was following what was happening as a definitely interested but non-interfering bystander.'

On subsequent occasions, the movement impulses developed and became more complex. Brad discovered that he could make a kind of inner gesture of permission, and the movement-impulses might or might not avail themselves of it. 'These movements formed series and patterns involving my whole body and my breathing too. These were not repetitive routines in which the same series and patterns would occur time after time. Basic movements occurred in different patterns, and in different series, lasting different lengths of time, and with differing degrees of muscle strain and intensity each time.'

What was happening to Brad? The answer, I believe, is simple. The effort to remain 'awake' had removed certain of his functions from the realm of the mechanical to the realm of the deliberate or controllable. Human beings are 99 per cent 'robot'. Our bodies are programmed to breathe, to sleep, to digest, to excrete; our instincts are programmed to reproduce our kind and protect our children. But our minds are also largely mechanical. A child has to learn to speak his own language; he then does it automatically, without effort. I can even learn to speak foreign languages without effort. I am typing this page without effort, because after thirty-odd years, typing has become 'automatic'. We *live* automatically. The answer to T.S. Eliot's question: 'Where is the life we have lost in living?' is: 'The robot has stolen it.'

It is, of course, extremely convenient to do so many things automatically; it saves me an immense amount of trouble. But it also robs me of a great deal of pleasure. When I first learned to drive, it was delightful to climb into a car and set it in motion – a feeling of astonishment and self-congratulation. I can still recapture that feeling if I make an enormous effort of imagination. It costs so much effort because I am having to wrest it from the hands of the robot.

The simplest way of ceasing to live 'mechanically' is to make a continual attempt at 'vigilance', self-awareness. From Brad's early diaries – dating back to his first days in Finland – it is clear that he had always made this effort to wrest a little freedom from the hands of the robot. In 1955, he wrote: 'Five years have gone by since I consciously began in this direction, and these traits which I hoped to get rid of are still with me.' And in 1958 he wrote:

> The learning and the teaching
> The fathering and the husbanding,
> this many-sided busyness cloaks a quiet waiting
> for the miracle to happen.

But it was the experience of years of stress and exhaustion that caused his own 'miracle' to happen.

The nights of waiting beside his son taught him the discipline of vigilance, of non-mechanical waiting. The 'robot' could not be allowed to take over; it had to be kept at bay. It happened again as he lay beside his wife during her long periods of schizophrenic 'absence'. And in pushing back the boundaries of his mechanicalness, he was extending the area of his freedom.

But the freedom applied to the right-brain 'self' as well as to the left. The right-brain entity is usually modest and self-effacing; it defers to the assertive left-brain ego. But as Brad's left-brain ego remained in suspension for hours at a time, the right began – with a certain hesitancy – to express itself. He gave it permission to continue. The result was the series of spontaneous movements.

And what was the right-brain self trying to achieve in these movements? The answer is to be found in his statement: 'My body was getting into better condition than it had been for a long time.' To a large extent, we drive our bodies with the will. Look at a man walking through the city with his briefcase; everything about him – his quick, firm walk, the way he leans forward slightly, the way he swings his umbrella – all testify to his purpose and his need to achieve maximum efficiency. It is completely different from his walk as he strolls home from a cricket match. The right brain prefers to do things slowly and easily, but the left is always in a hurry. Brad's right brain was saying, in effect: 'If you give me a chance, I'll show you how to relax properly and how to use your body properly. I'll show you how to perform your physical functions with a minimum of effort, and how to recover quickly from fatigue . . . .'

He records: 'The whole process became flowing and fluent as time went on. Furthermore, I could choose to slip into these movement experiences from much less intense levels of relaxation, and in an increasing variety of situations; for example, while sitting at my desk, sitting in an audience listening to someone lecture or in a theatre or concert hall; or standing at a bus stop waiting for a bus. For each situation I would choose limits to the kind of movements allowed so as not to draw

attention or become conspicuous. These limits did not at all
seem to prevent the process or lessen the quality of the experience for me.

'One of the first things I had noticed during the first few
weeks of these experiences was that I could trust my body to
move safely; that is, even though I usually had my eyes closed to
better concentrate, I never moved so as to fall off the bed, or hit
the wall or piece of furniture with some part of my body if I
were elsewhere in a room. . . .' The part of the mind that
enables a sleepwalker to stroll along the top of a wall without
falling off had surfaced in Brad when he was otherwise fully
conscious. He also noticed: 'Ordinary movements like walking,
sitting, getting up from a seated position, were not only getting
easier, but they were also changing. I found myself beginning to
choose to sit on hard chairs or seats, and to sit on the front part
of the seat with my back straight and lightly balanced. This did
not require any forceful conscious muscular efforts on my part;
it was not a disciplined effort – on the contrary, it was easier to
sit that way.'

One day, as he stood in the queue in the dining-room,
waiting to collect food from the buffet, he observed the now-
familiar impulse in his right hand and arm. He allowed the hand
to reach out towards the food. It went over the first plate, and
took a spoonful of food from the second plate. He relaxed and
waited; the arm again reached out and took food from another
plate. This continued until it had served the whole meal. The
choice of food surprised him. His hand reached for foods that he
had not touched for years. But there was no regular pattern. No
foods were totally ignored and none were regularly chosen. The
same held true of the amounts of food. 'Going to meals became
very exciting because I never knew beforehand what kind of
meal I would choose for myself. Sometimes, I would find myself
taking only a glass of sour milk or a glass of water, and, joining
the others who were eating, saying by way of explanation that
I did not seem hungry at the moment. Once I found myself
engaging in a complete fast, except for teas and juices and water,
and for five days I went to the dining-room for each meal, not
knowing if I would eat that meal or not.' But there was no

physical discomfort. As a result of this new way of eating, his weight, which had been between eighty-two and eighty-five kilograms, dropped by ten kilograms, and remained there.

Brad recalled an experiment in nutrition performed in the early fifties. Various types of food were placed on the floor, and infants were allowed to move among them and choose their own. After a short time – three or four weeks – the infants settled into a routine of eating which, according to the nutrition experts, was an ideal 'healthy diet'. Abraham Maslow had once cited a similar experiment; chickens were allowed to choose their own foods; but in this case, the un-nutritive food was flavoured with something that made it smell good, while the nutritive food smelt unappetizing. What emerged in this case was the observation that the *dominant* chickens – 5 per cent of the total – began to choose the nutritive food, in spite of its smell, while the non-dominant ones chose the appetizing food. The result was that the dominant chickens became even more dominant, while the non-dominant ones became less so. The lesson is plainly that the dominant creatures have a stronger instinct for the food which is best for them. But the baby experiment reveals that *all* human babies, both dominant and non-dominant, make an instinctive choice of what is good for them. The choice comes from what George Groddeck called the 'It', that something else inside us that seems to know what is best for us. In adults, this is always being overruled by the left-brain ego – and, in most cases, not for any sound reason. It is not good sense on *any* level when, because I am feeling tense, I gulp down a meal at top speed. It only gives me indigestion. And I may often *know* perfectly well that what I am doing is silly; my reason, which is closely connected to the left-brain ego, can see that quite clearly. So what is making me eat too fast? Not my reason, and certainly not my instinct, but a conglomeration that I can only call 'the false self'. Rather complicated feedback mechanisms are at work: my tension releases adrenalin into my system, and the adrenalin urges me to eat faster, even though I may feel that this is bad for me. My 'robot' then proceeds to develop bad eating habits; and if I become anxious about these, things may get worse than ever. What is necessary is quite obvious. The controlling 'I' has to assert itself, and set out to break the bad habits. It must cease to feel helpless and passive. For the final decisions always lie in the hands of this controlling ego.

Brad himself came to recognize this through an interesting experience. His wife was also beginning to experience spontaneous movements, and the two of them would sometimes allow these movements to integrate into patterns. 'Sometimes we found ourselves acting out non-verbal role playing in situations which also developed without conscious intent.'

Late one evening, Brad and his wife began a 'duet' of spontaneous movements. It developed into a situation in which he made sexual advances which she resisted. Brad allowed the impulses to continue, and began making increasingly strong assaults, until a kind of attempted rape developed. She continued to plead with him to stop; he made no attempt to check the impulse. Suddenly, his impulse collapsed, and they both felt frightened and bewildered. Brad began to wonder whether he could trust an impulse that had led to a near-rape. The next day, he telephoned a friend who had studied Zen Buddhism in Japan. Her reply was that no matter how much power and authority these impulses seemed to have, he must recognize that *he* was in charge. 'The part is not meant to dominate the whole.' His mistake had been to assume that this 'other self', which seemed to have a deeper insight into questions of health and diet, must be right about everything. In essence, her advice was: stop being so passive. This is only a part of you. Consult it by all means, but do not make it your sole guide and mentor.

My own interpretation of this episode would be that Brad's 'other self' was attempting to correct another kind of imbalance. I have never met anyone who struck me as less capable of rape than Brad. His whole personality is gentle, thoughtful, receptive. His early journals show continuous self-analysis and self-criticism. Yet all men need to be capable, at times, of expressing some degree of aggression, if only jokingly. Presumably the 'impulse' was trying to add a dash of sexual aggression to the totality of Brad's personality. . . .

In short, the 'It', the other self, is the regulator of the body and the instincts, what Gurdjieff called 'the moving centre'. It is, in short, the 'wisdom of the body'. And it has no real jurisdiction in the realm of the mind. Its task – when it is allowed to get on with it – is to maintain physical health and balance. Brad noticed this one day when he came back from his first ski of the winter; as he lay on the bed, his muscles aching, his leg muscles began making spontaneous movements in the opposite direction from the strains·he could feel in his muscles. In effect, they were saying: 'Don't just lie there waiting for the tiredness to go away; you can *do* something about it.' We have all noticed something of the sort. When very tired, the best way to unwind is not to lie down and try to relax; it is to get *absorbed* in something else. Five minutes' total absorption – let us say, in some fascinating news item on television – recharge our vital batteries more than hours of trying to relax.

Watching cats, dogs and babies in Viittakivi, Brad noticed how many of their movements seemed to have no obvious purpose. In adults, such spontaneous movements become restricted to yawning, stretching, rubbing the eyes, scratching, and a few others; but anyone can observe that pleasant ripple that flows along the muscles when we yawn and stretch, and how it is followed by relaxation.

Another important point to note is that most of us have no idea of how really to relax. The only time we do it 'properly' is when we have been anxious, and the anxiety disappears. Imagine a man lying out on his front lawn on a sunny day, reading the newspaper. Suddenly his wife looks out of the window and says: 'Is baby out there with you?', and he says: 'No', and jumps to his feet. For five minutes there is considerable tension as they rush out into the street and search the house – until they find baby asleep under the bed. And when he lies down in the sunlight again, he feels *really* relaxed; the relief almost makes him feel dizzy. Events like this make us aware that, even when we think we are relaxed, half our circuits are still switched on. Why? Because modern life gets us into a habit of 'vigilance', and we may become so accustomed to continuous movement that we never have time to 'unwind'.

But even this does not explain why I cannot relax when I

want to – when I am lying in the sunlight with nothing to do for the rest of the day. In order to understand this, we have to recognize that the real culprit is 'the robot', that automatic servant who becomes so accustomed to rushing that he begins to anticipate our wishes – or what he thinks are our wishes – and keeps us in a state of subconscious alertness all the time. When the robot has formed a habit, it can only be broken by determined conscious effort.

The widest and most prevalent example is boredom. When I prepare to engage in some interesting task, I generate a certain tension – another name for energy – and this tension is discharged as I perform the task. My robot, accustomed to non-stop activity, maintains a state of subconscious tension for most of the time. (I use subconscious here to denote the twilight realm between conscious and unconscious.) And his foresight is usually justified – life is always throwing up unexpected challenges. But if, for some reason, I have to sit quietly for a fairly long time – in a dentist's waiting-room, in an airport lounge, on a train – the tension begins to form a pool inside me. If we observe ourselves in a state of boredom, we note that it is a state of discomfort, like wanting to urinate badly.

The consciousness of modern man has an almost permanent substratum of this kind of discomfort – in other words, of boredom. When a crowd at a boxing match or a football game screams itself hoarse, it is deliberately discharging this tension. Football hooliganism is a simple and understandable extension of this method. The hooligan has just *seen* how satisfactorily he can discharge his tensions by cheering for his team, and his unconscious mind cannot understand why he should not extend this principle and display conspicuous gallantry in combat with the supporters of the other team, or against these 'civilian' shopkeepers and publicans who are not on one side or the other. . . . (All soldiers feel a patronizing contempt for non-combatants.)

This is the 'mechanical' method of discharging tension (boredom). But there is an alternative method: the method of conscious control. Imagine that you are about to set out on a long train journey – a journey that usually leaves you exhausted and shattered – and for some reason you are convinced you will have a serious accident. On the train, you sit and stare out of the window, wondering if today is your last. Every time the train brakes, you tense your muscles, waiting for the crash. Yet you never experience a single moment of boredom; and when you get off at your destination, you are surprised to feel as fresh as when you got on board. Maintaining continual alertness has prevented the robot from taking over. Moreover, when you finally settle down in an armchair to watch television, you sink into a deep and genuine relaxation, free of underlying tension. You have temporarily broken a bad habit. . . .

This is how Brad achieved total relaxation, lying at the side of his wife in a condition in which total alertness was combined with relaxation. His conscious mind undid the bad habits of a lifetime. As a result, he was launched into a totally new area of experience.

What had happened is that Brad had reconstituted the parliament of his mind, and given the Member for the Subconscious (or the right brain) wider powers of action. He immediately found one field of activity in which this wider power could be utilized. Bee-keeping had always been one of his major enthusiasms. His family was fond of honey, and Brad enjoyed the ritualistic aspect of the work. He would first take a shower, to lessen body odour – bees are understandably highly sensitive to smells, since they detect flowers by their sense of smell. He would don the protective clothing, like an astronaut. Then the opening of the hives would be performed like a slow-motion ballet, so as not to alarm or disturb the bees. Even before the movements started, Brad derived deep satisfaction from tending his bees; after a morning of slow-motion activity, he would lose all sense of time. He had slowed down the left brain until it worked at the same pace as the right. And, according to Sperry's observations, the right brain has very little sense of time. After the 'movements' began, he found that he could enter into the ritual of bee-keeping with a new sensitivity. Before he approached the hives, he would stand there, and engage in an inner dialogue. 'I am consciously aware of various factors that should influence my decisions about my work with the bees.

But I know I am also subconsciously aware of many other factors. In years of experience, I have noticed many things that have influenced my behaviour towards the bees; I must allow these to influence my decisions today. I have also forgotten many things; it would be good if these too could influence my behaviour. . . .' And, with this ritual dialogue completed, he would wait for the movement impulses to take over, and then allow them to carry out his work with the bees. He never quite decided whether this new method increased the output of honey. The only thing that was quite certain was that this way of working was deeply satisfying, a way of entering the situation with his whole being, like a man wading into the sea.

Another experience of this period underlines an important aspect of these movements. During a flu epidemic, Brad had to spend several days in bed. Lying there on a Sunday afternoon, completely relaxed, he allowed the movement impulses to take over. They led him out of bed and into the kitchen, where he found himself putting the kettle on to boil, and then – moving very slowly – choosing certain dishes, arranging them on the tray, placing a decorative centrepiece in their midst, preparing the tea, carrying the tray to the carpeted floor of the living room, and there sitting down and going through a stylized tea-drinking ceremony. He had seen the tea ceremony performed in that same room by a Japanese student; but this was not at all the same thing. He was struck by the thought that perhaps the original tea ceremonies had originated in this way. In fact, the Japanese tea ceremonies, like their rock gardens, are designed to create a state of inner calm which will allow the emergence of such subconscious impulses.

The next stage of this development was yet more interesting, and raises important questions. One day when Brad was sitting at the tea table, drinking a third cup of tea and feeling relaxed and sleepy, his little daughter asked him to make a drawing that she could colour. When Brad said he was too sleepy, she left the pencil and paper, and went off to play. He felt the familiar impulse in his arm, and watched his hand move out to pick up the pencil. It drew a line, relaxed, then drew another line, and went on until the drawing was finished. It was a curious, flower-like pattern. The next day, after work, he took some oil-pastel crayons, relaxed into a state of receptive readiness, and again watched his hand take up crayons and create an exotic fantasy flower. This continued for the next two weeks, flower after flower, all quite different.

Brad brought a folder of his drawings along to our chalet, and I found them fascinating. I have a box of colour transparencies of them beside me as I write, and even in this much-reduced form, I find them very striking. Each one is a beautiful, elaborate and complete pattern, virtually a completed painting. Two of them resemble Paul Klee fish (many people who have seen them have this impression of Paul Klee fantasy at first glance). I imagine that Klee was giving expression to the same deep pattern-making impulses of the subconscious. They are all very elaborate, and deeply satisfying to look at. A bad painting or drawing, like a bad piece of writing, seems too crude and obvious – so much more obvious than life. A good painting has some satisfying complexity that makes it resemble life. Brad's colour drawings all have this complexity. Although they all look like small fragments of various – and totally different – patterns, they are quite unlike, say, the design of a carpet, which is repetitive. These seem to be designs caught in flight as they rush through the mind, expanding into other designs with the infinite variety of the unconscious. Some look like glimpses of space with exploding stars, some like a shower of multi-coloured eyeballs, some like strange angular birds, some like Douanier Rousseau flowers, some like creatures seen under a microscope, some like curious abstract paintings. To my mind, they are the most striking of the products of his 'impulses', for they could not be faked. They leave no doubt that the subconscious self knew precisely what it was doing. They are instant, visual evidence that something very strange took place. Their variety seems enormous; they could be reproduced in a book, and would be as visually satisfying as the work of most modern painters; moreover, they give the impression of coming from an inexhaustible supply, as if Brad could have gone on producing one a day for ten years without repeating himself.

The first dozen or so drawings were produced in less than

two weeks, and then Brad temporarily 'dried up'. He felt that it was a pity to allow this ability to slip away, and tried nudging it into activity. The impulses began again, but this time the results seemed to be a crude, mocking caricature of the previous drawings, and he had a strong feeling that something was wrong. He found himself saying to himself: 'All right, I get the message – I will not force myself to draw.' And he stopped. Six months later, the impulse returned; he bought a pack of colour felt-pens, and began again, this time producing another seventy-two in about eighteen months. As he did them, he had a sense of watching a stranger at work. In some cases, he would criticize: 'My God, how can that colour possibly go with the others?' But the stranger always knew best. Finally came two particularly fine drawings which he labelled 'The fireball' and 'The ice crystal'. These seemed to have a quality of finality, like a period at the end of a sentence. It was as if some inner territory had been completely mapped. The drawing impulse then disappeared, except for two small 'epilogue' drawings.

This drawing period raises more questions than I can fully discuss in a short book. The drawings resemble 'psychedelic patterns', but they were not produced under any kind of drug. This suggests that the patterns seen by patients who have taken mescalin, LSD or one of the other mind-changing drugs are in some way 'objective' parts of some inner landscape – perhaps Jung's 'archetypes of the collective unconscious'. In my book *Mysteries* I discuss the Frenchman René Daumal, who attempted to explore his 'inner world' by holding a handkerchief soaked with ether against his nostrils; when he began to lose consciousness, his hand would fall and he would recover. In this way he hoped to snatch glimpses of his unconscious mind. He had an overwhelming sense of meanings flashing by at a pace too fast to pin down, 'an instantaneous and intense world of eternity, a concentrated flame of reality', a vision of circles and triangles moving and combining in an inexpressibly complex manner, and a sound like a ritual chant or formula. Daumal speaks of a vision of curved non-Euclidian space and time.

Again, in a remarkable book called *A Drug Taker's Notes*, R. H. Ward speaks of his experiences under dental gas, and later with LSD25. He speaks of the sensation of passing, after a few whiffs of gas, 'into a state of consciousness already far more complete than the fullest degree of ordinary waking consciousness'. Again, he gives pages of description of his experience of these inner realms. There are dozens of similar experiences on record, leaving no possible doubt that our ordinary consciousness is of an extremely inferior and limited variety, like looking at a scene through a crack in a fence, and that the 'inner realm' *is* a genuinely objective realm, not a subjective world of dreams and delusions. In a state of mental stress just before the First World War, Jung learned how to descend, consciously, into this inner realm – a trick he called 'active imagination' – and described his experiences in detail in his autobiography *Memories, Dreams, Reflections*. (And again, I have discussed these at length in *Mysteries*, particularly in the chapter called 'Descent into the Unconscious'.)

At the moment, we know as little of these inner realms as William the Conqueror knew about the world beyond Europe. It was only in the 1950s that Aldous Huxley first clearly formulated this notion that the inner realm is as vast, as real and as strange as the globe upon which we live. One day, when future Columbuses and Vasco da Gamas have provided accurate maps of the New Worlds of our minds, we shall re-read Jung, R. H. Ward, René Daumal, John Lilly, and be able to specify just what part of this *terra incognita* was explored in their pioneer inner voyages. And when that happens, I think we shall also look at Brad's drawings, and recognize that each one is as precise and significant as the formulae of relativity or quantum mechanics. When I spoke of them with Brad, he described his own feeling that the 'someone' who made them was trying to tell him things which could only be expressed in this way. I also have an obscure sense of a meaning slightly beyond my grasp as I look at them – but not, as with music, because there is no exact verbal equivalent; rather, because they are glimpses of a pattern that I have never seen as a whole.

But even if we are inclined to reject all this as mysticism, at least it cannot be doubted that the drawings reveal the 'other' part of the brain as a reservoir of pure creativity. This was equally obvious when I looked at some of Brad's 'metal sculptures'. He brought them along at the same time as the drawings, and at first I was dazzled by the almost oriental intricacy of the patterns. They were all made out of the same kind of scrap metal – sheets of 'leftovers' after holes had been punched out, leaving a lattice or grid made up of connected triangles. It seemed unbelievable that so many patterns could be made out of anything so simple – by comparison, my younger son's 'Rubik snake' is crude and obvious. Brad said that he was equally surprised; he had simply watched his hands bending the metal with a pair of pliers, and had no idea of what would emerge. Obviously, what had happened was that the pattern-making department of his brain – the right hemisphere – had succeeded in taking over his hands, and expressing its ideas without any kind of interference from the critical faculty. And this in itself is something of a miracle. As I write these words, the meanings of what I intend to say emerge from my right brain, and my left catches them and clothes them in words. After years of practice, it does this quite competently. And unless my left brain performed its part of the operation, the meaning would simply remain unexpressed. Even artists and musicians and ballet dancers have to use the intermediary of the left hemisphere to select and filter their spontaneous impulses. If the left is feeling tired, or intervenes too actively (out of nervousness or self-consciousness) the communication becomes jammed, and a kind of stutter emerges. (Stuttering itself is the most commonplace example of excessive interference of the left brain with right-brain functions.) We all know that we do these things best if we do them without too much self-consciousness. Michael Polanyi pointed out that a pianist who concentrated on his fingers would play badly. He must attend *from* his fingers, *to* the music.

Here is the basic insight into the whole problem discussed in the opening chapter – the problem of 'alienation', the feeling of 'absurdity', 'nausea', futility and meaninglessness. They all involve attending *to* something instead of attending *from* it. Sartre's 'nausea', in the novel of that title, is due to looking at the tree and nothing but the tree – failing to see beyond it to the wood. A stutter is like a brake that keeps catching on the wheel, making it shudder. In 'nausea', the brake has locked completely.

What Brad achieved was the equivalent of a wheel without a brake. The stutterer cannot *help* interfering with his natural self-expression, even though he would greatly prefer not to interfere; the interference has become automatic, robotic. Brad had succeeded in persuading his left brain to adopt a policy of total non-interference. Betty Edwards's book *Drawing on the Right Side of the Brain* describes various tricks for persuading the left brain to stop interfering. She points out that many sketches of familiar objects are bad because we *know* too much about the object, and try to put this knowledge into the drawing. If someone looks at the object through a simple 'view-finder', and concentrates on its mere *shape*, ignoring all other data, the result is a far more accurate drawing. Brad's hours of 'suspended consciousness', lying beside his wife, were a far more effective method of preventing left-brain interference.

The next stage was the writing of the poetry – or rather, the 'concentrates'. But before we discuss these, another experience of the same period should be mentioned.

'One morning, in my study, movement-impulse writing began, but the handwriting that took form on the page was completely foreign to me – it was not like my handwriting at all. I do not remember the sentence word for word, but it was a sentence in which a person, who named herself, briefly introduced herself. I looked at the sentence in amazement. Always, up to now, I had felt quite clearly that my movement-impulse writing was expressing various levels of myself. Strong rejecting feelings filled me completely. I put the pencil down, pushed the paper away, and found myself saying with a tone of uncompromising determination: "I . . . will . . . not . . . be . . . a . . . mouthpiece . . . for . . . anyone . . . but . . . myself!" '

This is important, because it makes it clear that Brad recognized 'movement-impulses' as a part of himself. (This, justifies his own deliberate reshaping of some of the 'concentrates'.) Many modern investigators in the field of psychical research are inclined to believe that all 'automatic writing' is simply an expression of the unconscious mind of the writer. Brad's experience clearly contradicts this view. On this one occasion, he recognized the 'entity' as *another person* who wanted to join in the dialogue. He concludes, 'There was never a repetition of that kind of experience.'

This explains, then, why the 'concentrates' were less spontaneous than the drawings or metal sculptures. Among Brad's notes, I see many early poems dating from his earliest years in Finland, and these have that same quality of photographic observation that is found in the concentrates:

> The black glass-smooth lake with its cold shine
> breathes a whispy mist
> That makes the far shore tree groups into dark,
> solitary islands.

And he admits that the writing period began as a result of conscious meditation upon the theme, 'What are words?' But the process followed the familiar pattern. The impulse in his arm would lead him to pick up a pencil and allow his hand to write, one word at a time, without thinking about it. Then he would read the words, and try to understand the meaning. He would then attempt to express this meaning more clearly, making sentences around key words. If the writing reached an impasse, he would relax and allow the 'automatic writing' to take over again. This was clearly much more of a collaboration between the 'two selves'. But then, I find it difficult to envisage writing which is not such a collaboration. Sperry's experiments showed that although the right brain understands language, its linguistic capacities are poor compared with those of the left, just as most of us write very badly with the left hand (connected to the right brain) compared to the right. Here, it seems to me, the images are moving closer to the world of our conscious understanding. Reading Brad's concentrates, I am often reminded of the musical landscapes in the symphonies of Bruckner, or of the peaceful visionary landscapes in the paintings of my friend William Arkle. When man wishes to express the impersonal, he turns to nature. It is the same with the German romantic writer of *novelle*, Adalbert Stifter. His stories are usually simple, like folk tales; they could be told in a few paragraphs. But he devotes page after page to descriptions of natural scenery, or explanations about local customs. A critical student might accuse him of padding. But the perceptive reader soon recognizes that, far from being 'padding', these descriptions of hills, mountains, forests, lakes, are in a sense more important than the story itself. J.P. Stern says of him: 'We feel he would rather not tell the story at all. . . .' Stifter is escaping from his personal self through these descriptions of scenery. And this is surely the heart of the matter. For what he is escaping *to* is not simply the impersonal world of nature, but his own inner mountain landscape.

This seems to me to be the essence of the longest and most important of Brad's concentrates – the one that led to the writing of this book:

> Following the afterimage of a wise old man within me
> I walked a road within me,
> up over forested ridges
> down through meadowed valleys,
> to a dead end
> that became a lane, and then a path
> leading towards a muffled roar
> growing louder and louder within me
> to where the path opened out
> of the tangly bushes
> into a spacious green glen,
> and beyond the glen . . .
> the roar itself.
> Breaking through the shorelines of a calm upper lake
> overflow waters were rushing down
> boulder strewn, rock studded
> irregular channels
> forming,
> swirling, slashing,
> curling, crashing
> rapids within me.
>
> Nearby,
> in the dense underbrush surrounding the glen

lay mossgrown millstones
    worn smooth by wear and weather, memorials of a mill
    once working within me,
    its mechanical being turning the power
    from swirling rushing rapids
    to revolving stones
    grinding the seeds of harvests.

Within the glen,
    near the rapids bank, was a solitary tree
    of gigantic girth and stature. . . .

widely spreading, deeply probing roots
drawing up the overflow into their growth,
stabilizing the earth along the bank;
    leaves of widely spreading
    highly reaching branches,
    drawing down the sun into their growth,
    releasing refreshment into the air . . .
an organic power transformer
    outliving the mill
    within me.

Downstream, to my right,
    the rushing rapids eased
    into a smooth even flow
    that slowly stilled
    into the calm serene being
    of new found depths.

I left the rapids and the glen within me,
still following the afterimage of the wise old man,
    back along the path that became a lane
    that led to the road end, now beginning,
    down through the meadowed valleys,
    up over forested ridges, all familiar now,
to a point where a path appeared
in the dense forest along the road.

I walked this path right off the road
    through the thick tree screen,
and suddenly, up before my eyes
stood revealed through thinning trees
the steep mossy slope of a forested mountain.

The path led up irregularly . . .
    around stumps and stones,
    through dead leaves, branches,
    and low bushes with wintered berries,
    hanging dull and red here and there . . .
until high up, upon the slope,
I reached an open clearing around a granite boulder
which I climbed
to look back over whence I had come . . .
    the forests, the ridges,
    the meadows and valleys
    just travelled through.

There, beyond them,
lay the calm deep waters
that were stilling the rushing rapids
of the overflow within me.
Contrasting patches
of dark purple cloud shadows
and glistening radiant sunlight
moved over land and the peaceful waters,
and islands rose reflected
from its still serene surface.
And along the distant skyline of the far shores
rose hazy silhouettes of other forested regions yet unreached.

This concentrate excited me because it was such a striking example of Jung's 'active imagination', or of the kabbalistic technique of inner travel. But there was another reason, connected with my own experiences of tension and 'panic'. I had – as described earlier – identified the root of the trouble as the 'emotional body', a kind of spoilt child that hides inside all of us, and whose separate identity only becomes obvious in times of misery or fear, when he becomes uncontrollable. Now in writing the book on the poltergeist, I had returned to the books of Max Freedom Long on the Hunas of Hawaii, for Huna 'magicians' (called *kahunas*) seem to be able to cause appalling damage, even death, by somehow making magical use of 'poltergeists'. But what interested me so much about the Hunas was their belief that man has no less than three souls or 'selves', which they call the *unihipili*, the *uhane* and the *aumakua*, meaning 'low self', 'middle self' and 'high self'. When Max Freedom Long first went to Hawaii as a young man, he become so intrigued by the strange beliefs of the Hunas that he tried hard to penetrate their secrets. He began with the etymology of these three Hawaiian words, and concluded that *unihipili*, low self, means a spirit which can grieve but may not be able to talk. *Uhane*, middle self, means a spirit which can talk. And Long quickly became convinced that these two 'souls' correspond quite exactly to our western notions of the conscious and unconscious minds. (He rather loosely uses the term 'subconscious', which I use to mean the twilight realm between the two, so I shall refer to the *unihipili* as the unconscious.)

Long goes on: 'To summarize, the *kahuna* idea of the conscious and subconscious seems to be, judging from the root meaning of the names given them, a pair of spirits closely joined in a body which is controlled by the subconscious and used to cover and hide them both. The conscious spirit is more human and possesses the ability to talk. The grieving subconscious weeps tears, dribbles water, and otherwise handles the vital force of the body. It does its work with secret and silent care, but it is stubborn and is disposed to refuse to obey.'

My panic attacks had made me very familiar with that refusal to obey, which led me to compare the *unihipili* – which I called the emotional body – to T. E. Lawrence's camel refusing to go back into the desert. I was also deeply struck by Long's remark that the *unihipili* 'intermingles with or tinctures the conscious spirit to give the impression of being one with it'. That is most certainly true. The emotional body is so dangerous because I think it *is* 'me'. When the emotional body goes into revolt, I feel completely shattered and undermined because it seems to me that *I* am betraying myself. Lawrence remarks in the *Seven Pillars* that during the desert war, he saw men drive themselves to the limits of endurance, yet there was never a sign of a break *unless it came from within*. When the mind is unified and confident in purpose, nothing can go wrong. When the emotional body becomes hysterical, then and only then are we in danger of inner defeat. This is the basic explanation of all mental illness and of all suicide.

Now, the chief characteristic of the *uhane* (middle self) is that it can *talk*, which reminds us that this function is governed by the left brain. And we have already seen that this left-brain self is the 'everyday self', the consciousness that confronts the world, the being who 'copes' with human existence. This notion is confirmed by Enid Hoffman's book, *Huna: A Beginner's Guide*, in a chapter called 'The selves in the brain'. She remarks: 'The middle self, whose consciousness is centred in the left hemisphere of the cortex . . . of the brain, continually reviews the information coming from the low self, whose consciousness is centred in the solar plexus.' And this identification of the 'dwelling place' of the *unihipili* also seems to make sense. When we are in an upset and undermined condition, we keep on feeling a 'sinking sensation' in the pit of the stomach.

So the spoilt schoolboy lives in the solar plexus, and the 'middle self' lives in the left brain. Then what of the right brain? According to Enid Hoffman's interpretation of the *kahunas*, *this* is the home of the 'high self', the *aumakua*. According to the *kahunas*, the high self knows the future and can control it. If the *unihipili* is our unconscious 'basement', then the *aumakua* is the superconscious 'attic'. The main difference between the unconscious and the superconscious is that we can, if we relax deeply, allow the activities of the unconscious to enter consciousness. But the activities of the superconscious are normally inaccessible to us. We can, according to the *kahunas*, communicate with the 'high self' (and so control our own futures), but it has to be done *via* the 'low self'. The telephone line from the middle self runs via the low self; there is no direct line to the superconscious.

One obvious consequence is that if the 'low self' is in a state of misery and revolt – as mine was during the panic attacks – then no messages can get through to the superconscious; there is too much crackling on the line. If we wish to make use of the superconscious, the first step is to soothe the unconscious into serenity.

If the unconscious is a spoilt schoolboy, then what symbol would be appropriate for the superconscious? I had already decided, before I read Brad's poem, that it was the wise old man of Jung's inner voyages. So Brad's poem fell upon ground that was perfectly prepared for it.

I asked Brad how he had come to write the poem, and his explanation confirmed my feeling that it was a communication of the *aumakua*. In June 1976, he began to experience a feeling of restlessness and a need to be alone. By now, he recognized the symptoms well enough to know that he had to find the time and the patience to allow something to surface. He telephoned friends who lived in a remote part of central Finland, Bob and Beverley Schrader, and asked if he could go and spend a few days with them. On the evening of his arrival, Beverley mentioned that she had recently discovered an interesting piece of scenery on one of her walks. The next morning, Brad set off on the walk she had recommended. 'During the whole walk I sensed everything with slow, intensive concentration – not thinking about it, but just taking it all in very deeply. Everything about that walk felt significant and important in some inexplicable way.' The following day, he accompanied Bob Schrader on a walk in the opposite direction, and again experienced the same sense of significance, of something rising slowly to the surface. By the next morning, he knew that his purpose had been achieved; the walks had accomplished the release of the impulse that had made him restless. He was able to write the 'concentrate'. 'With the writing completed, I felt that it stood in the same relationship to me and my inner world as my last two paintings had: i.e. that it was a summarized account of the way I had come in my recent personal development, a concentrated synthesis of my inner state of being, a symbolic map of the fundamental features of my inner territory, and an integrated presentation of my past, present and future direction.'

The meaning of the symbolism need not at present concern us: the overflowing lake, the rapids, the now-defunct mill, the great tree whose roots hold the bank together, the forested slopes of the mountain, the clearing with the granite boulder, the calm waters of the pool. An 'explained' symbol is a symbol drained of half its meaning. But the poem leaves us facing a far more important question: in fact, the question that lies at the centre of this book: what was Brad's 'wise old man', his *aumakua*, trying to tell him? The implications are so complex that they require a chapter to themselves.

4

The Road to Visionary Consciousness

The question needs to be considered in stages: the 'movements', the 'tea ceremony', the 'bee-hive ceremony', the metal sculptures, the paintings, the concentrates.

We have already seen that the purpose of the original movements seemed to be to improve Brad's physical condition, to reduce his weight to its natural level, to teach him to make proper use of his energies and powers of recuperation. Once this had been achieved, it seems to have moved on to a more constructive or creative stage. The emphasis shifted from the body to the mind. The mind of modern man flows forward like a narrow, fast stream; it needs to be taught to broaden into a slow-flowing river. Brad's 'tea ceremony' seems to have been an attempt to show him that even a simple, functional activity like making tea could be given a third dimension of meaning, turning it literally into a ritual – after all, the purpose of all religious ritual is to re-awaken the memory of something that we ought never to forget. The same is true of the 'bee-hive ceremony'. Brad had always performed his work with the bees in a slow and deliberate manner, because bees respond better to slow movement. The 'wise old man' said, in effect: 'Why waste this activity? Why not make it an opportunity for communion with the rest of your being?' And so tending the bees became another religious ritual.

The paintings and metal sculptures represent a new level of creativity. What surprised me most about the metal sculptures was their astonishing variety. I would not have believed it possible to make so many elaborate and beautiful shapes from those strips of triangular metal. To do so required what Edward de Bono calls 'lateral thinking'. Again, we fail to see these possibilities because our minds rush forward in a straight line. In causing Brad's hands to make these elaborate shapes, the *aumakua* was attempting to show him all the hidden possibilities that were being overlooked by that over-purposeful left brain. It was saying in plain language: 'You are *overlooking* half the meaning of the world that surrounds you. Slow down. Learn to "stand and stare".'

The paintings take us a stage further, with their distinctly 'psychedelic' air, and we know that psychedelic drugs such as mescalin have the effect of disconnecting our obsessive left-brain consciousness, which treats the world as if it were a mere diagram, and making us conscious of its immense, solid, self-sustaining reality. The coloured stripes on Aldous Huxley's deck chair seemed to become stripes of fire. When mescalin-takers close their eyes, they see coloured shapes very much like those painted by Brad. I have already mentioned the similarity to some of the paintings of Paul Klee. Are these paintings a reflection of some strange geometry of our inner world, such as that glimpsed by René Daumal? The most obvious thing about Brad's paintings is that every one of them is clearly a fragment of something larger; not one has an air of self-completeness.

I am here reminded of a very remarkable book, *Essay on the Origin of Thought* by Jurij Moskvitin, which deserves to be far better known. Published by Ohio University Press in 1974 – my copy was sent to me by some unknown well-wisher -- it seems to have been more-or-less stillborn.

Moskvitin describes how one day, lying in the sunlight with his eyes half-closed, he was observing the colour spectrum that sometimes becomes visible when the eyelashes partly cover the eyes. Then, he says: 'Suddenly I became aware as if of a film in the background, a screen or a mosaic with the most strange and beautiful patterns which gave me the feeling of watching something particularly significant'. These patterns were constantly moving and changing, and seemed to be made of several layers or screens moving behind each other. 'Sometimes the patterns became like an embroidery of small interconnected swastikas, sometimes combinations of triangles and meandering ornaments. . . .' And as he gradually developed the ability to focus upon these patterns, he recognized their similarity to patterns in religious art, or 'art and ornamentation created by civilizations dominated by mystical initiation and experience'. The forms began to suggest figures of the physical world, but always highly stylized, like Mexican masks. The patterns changed into other patterns when some rows of the 'mosaic' seemed to become prominent, to stand out. Studying these, he became convinced that they were made up of 'dancing sparks' of the kind sometimes seen in migraine. He compared the effect to a painting by the *'pointilliste'* painter Signac, and began to believe that our normal visual field is actually made up of these sparks, although we do not normally focus on them.

Moskvitin's next observation was that the sparks had tiny tails, like comets or tadpoles, and that the sparks and their tails seemed to be part of something larger – smoke-like forms floating in the air. He compares the effect to a Dutch painting in which a beautiful wine glass, on closer observation, proves to be simply a few dashes of yellow paint. In other words, we *impose* our own meanings on these smoke-like forms, rather as you can rub your eyes until you see flashes of colour behind your eyelids, and then cause these splashes to change into various shapes as your daydreams or thoughts somehow mingle with them. He says: 'The forms came floating out of anything I looked at, lying like cobwebs around all objects, and from these stretching into my eyes, *as if the objects emanated from me*' (my italics).

Moskvitin's way of expressing his ideas is often obscure, and needs translating into simpler terminology. Here, for example, is one of his key sentences:

'If we remember that the essential difference between what we call the real world and the world of imagination and hallucination is not the elements of which we build them up but the sequence in which these elements appear – at random or directed by the sequence of external impulses – then it follows that the sequences directed from without represent a limitation of the otherwise unlimited combinations of the selective forms released at random from within.'

The last part of the sentence offers a flash of his meaning. We can see that Brad's paintings seem to suggest unlimited 'inner forms', a patterned world of infinite variety; Moskvitin is saying that the external world that our eyes reveal to us is just a limited version of that larger inner world. So he is saying here that these ghostly or smoke-like forms in some way *constitute* the external world (at least, as seen by our eyes). They can be 'constituted' in two ways: either from within – as when I rub my eyes and make the colours alter their shapes – or from without. What he seems to mean is that the world outside us arouses in us certain stock responses, certain expectations, and these shape the 'forms' into the familiar objects of the world.

A simple way of grasping his meaning is to think of the Rorschach test in which the patient is asked to look at a shapeless ink-blot and tell the psychiatrist what it reminds him of. Or of the way we can stare into a fire or at the clouds and see various faces and shapes. It is obvious there that we are selecting certain elements in the cloud or the inkblot, and then projecting our own expectations or visions *into* it.

Now Moskvitin is suggesting that, without being aware of it, we constantly 'project' a ghostly substance made of pinpoints of light on to the external world, just like the cloud or inkblot, and then project our expectations into it. I might reply: 'Nonsense. I *know* I am now seeing a tree.' But then, you might say, 'I *know* I am now seeing a glass' when I look at the Dutch painting; but a closer look shows me that it is merely a few streaks of paint, which on close examination do not even look like a glass.

All this sounds highly speculative and mystical – particularly later in the book, when Moskvitin speaks about the mystic Plotinus, who seems to feel that we somehow 'project' the real world from deep inside the soul, as if the soul were a cinema projector and the world was merely a blank screen. In fact, Moskvitin's ideas are simply an interesting variation on the basic insights of the philosopher Edmund Husserl. Husserl's basic recognition is that perception is *intentional*. We tend to think, when we see something, that it simply walks in through our eyes and is grasped by the brain. But even this way of expressing the idea gives the show away. For if I happen to be day-dreaming, or thinking of something else, then I do *not* grasp what I happen to be looking at, and as a result, I do not see it. If I look at my watch without paying attention, I do not see the time – or rather, I do not grasp it, and I have to look a second time with my attention awake. In order to perceive something I must reach out and grasp it, just as I pick up a book in my hand.

This insight sounds commonplace enough – hardly the basis for a revolutionary new philosophy of perception. But as soon as we know that we have to *grasp* actively for what we see, we also know that we can look at something with full attention and still not see its essential meaning because we are not attempting to grasp it. As far as I can make out, the television means absolutely nothing to my dog; he is not even interested in *Lassie Come Home.* I suspect that he simply sees it as moving shapes on a screen, just like the movements of clouds – quite meaningless, because he does not grasp the sense in it.

In the same way, two people can look at an urban landscape of deserted factories against a background of muddy junk-yards, and experience totally different reactions. One of them shudders and thinks: 'How dreary.' The other, who happens to be an industrial archaeologist, thinks: 'How fascinating.'

But this is not simply a difference of *opinion.* One is putting far more *into* it than the other. If we could get behind the eyes of the two men, we would realize that one of them sees a dull, poorly-defined landscape, like a smudgy photograph, while the other sees something more like a great painting. The industrial archaeologist's picture is sharp, clear, full of satisfying colours and shapes. In short, he is seeing the landscape with a kind of 'mescalin vision'. And he is doing this by *grasping* more of it.

What Moskvitin is saying is that when we 'see' something, we actually *paint* it. Seeing is an instantaneous act of painting, and the paintbrush is this magical rush of 'sparks' from our eyes. He is not, of course, saying that the world 'out there' does not really exist. He seems to be saying that it is infinitely more beautiful and complex than we can ever grasp. He remarks:

'Our situation is somewhat that of a horse or dog trained to perform tasks far beyond its natural capacities.' And we can easily see that if my dog walks into a library, it simply does not see the same library that I see, for the books have no significance whatever for a dog. But I am prepared to believe that when we go for walks, I do not see the world that he sees, for his sense of smell and his interest in rabbits, foxes, birds and other creatures makes his view of nature far richer and more complex than mine. But when he walks into my library, his eyes 'paint' it in a few strokes.

To put this another way: our experience of the world is like listening to a piece of music. When I was a child, all classical music sounded much the same to me – an endless blur of noise. As I grew up, I gradually learned to recognize features in this blur, until now I can tell whether I am listening to a good or bad performance of a Brahms symphony. Anyone can see that it would be nonsense to say that the child hears the same Brahms symphony as an adult. And I can only tell a good from a bad performance because I know the symphony well enough to create my *own* symphony as I listen, and compare my mental version with the one being played. We 'create' the world we see in the same sense.

Husserl used to refer to this 'creative self' as the transcendental ego. This is the 'painter'. But when he paints a Brahms symphony, the painter is limited by the symphony as Brahms actually wrote it. When he paints a tree or a landscape, he is limited by his knowledge of real trees and landscapes. But when he uses that strange, magic 'smoke' inside his head, he is far less limited. He can create his own symphonies and patterns.

Yet even if I happen to be a great composer or painter, my work remains somehow limited. Every artist knows what it means to 'lack inspiration'; it means that the external world, the real world, seems to hold him in chains. He tries to create, but he can only observe. This is largely the fault of the left brain. Yet if he closes his eyes and begins to drift into a light sleep, his creativity is released in the forms of images and feelings; he may wake up after a few minutes completely refreshed and ready for work.

So the sheer profusion of patterns in Brad's paintings could be regarded as the right brain demonstrating its freedom from the limitations of the left. It is saying to the left-brain ego: 'I am here. Do not leave me out of account. Do not imagine that, when you confront the world, you are alone. I am always waiting in the background. . . .'

The question of why the paintings look like the familiar psychedelic patterns is at present unanswerable; Moskvitin's explanation seems as good as any: because the 'creative self', the transcendental ego, is a pattern-maker by profession, and he works in primary colours. We may assume that, if he had felt so inclined, he could have gone on and produced a thousand paintings, all completely different from one another.

This left brain, whose development has enabled man to ascend the evolutionary ladder quicker than any known species, has ended by impeding our further development. If Husserl and Moskvitin are right – or rather, *because* they are right – I am actually the creator of this world I see in front of me. That is not to say, of course, that I am the creator of the *real* world – that is something different again. *But of this representation which I take to be 'reality', and which is actually a 'painting', I am undoubtedly the creator.* Yet, trapped in my left-brain sense of identity, I fail to realize this. From the moment I am old enough to begin to take an interest in the reality around me, I believe that it is 'real', quite independent of me. When I feel ecstatically happy at Christmas, and when it seems self-evident to me that this world is infinitely richer and more marvellous than I had suspected, I believe that I am happy merely because it happens to be Christmas. If, a few days later, I remember the 'vision' of Christmas day, and wonder why the world has returned to its usual dullness, I feel that this is because my senses are too feeble, my powers of memory too weak, to maintain the vision. So I become convinced of a double lie: that I am rather weak and mediocre, and that my moments of happiness and vision are due entirely to circumstance.

Fortunately, healthy people experience almost daily flashes of 'vision' – the peak experience – which make us aware that there is something badly wrong with our basic assumptions; they bring the flash of 'absurd good news'. The sexual orgasm floods the senses with energy, and again, we experience the surge of confidence, the certainty of strength. In these moments we see, in a flash, how untrue it is that 'the world is what it is'. We see that our optimism, our determination, our will-power, can transform it.

This transformation can be accomplished in three ways. The first is the least satisfactory: we manipulate the senses. Drugs and alcohol will 'transform' the world. And so will giving yourself some 'reward' – buying yourself something expensive, taking a holiday. But these methods leave us trapped in the old fallacy: that we are weak and mediocre and that moments of happiness and vision are due to outside circumstance.

The second method is the one adopted by most human beings who are determined to evolve: the method of knowledge, of learning new things. Imagine that a dog has the potential intelligence of a human being, and that I want to make him aware that a library is a far more interesting place than he realizes. I would have to deepen his knowledge, make him grasp the function of language, then of writing, and so on. And the dog's mental painting of the library would acquire depth, a kind of third dimension of reality. In the same way, I deepen my perception of reality by adding to my knowledge. I may, for example, deepen my perception of a game of Rugby football or chess by learning its rules, so I can appreciate what is happening. I may deepen my perception of music by learning about its structure and its history. Science itself is a continual deepening of perception of the world. A really important and exciting idea may simply deepen one's perception of *everything*, as every religious convert knows.

The third method is the most difficult in practice, although the most simple in conception. This is actually to learn to grasp the creative function of the 'creative self'. To judge by his philosophy – a kind of mystical Platonism – Plotinus had succeeded; he recognized that the soul is the creator of the world. William Blake also seems to have succeeded. He says in his catalogue to *Vision of the Last Judgement*: 'The nature of visionary fancy, or imagination, is very little known, and the eternal nature and permanence of its ever existent images is considered as less permanent than the things of vegetative and generative nature . . . ,' and again: 'This world of imagination is the world of eternity; it is the divine bosom into which we shall all go after the death of the vegetated body. This world of imagination is infinite and eternal. . . .' He has recognized that this inner being, which creates works of art and literature, is also the Great Painter of the universe as we know it. And although it does not 'know' the real universe, this is really a relative matter. That 'real' world is simply far more rich and complex than we can grasp. And if we know this, and continue to expand our ability to grasp its complexity, then we have nothing to feel ashamed about. The damned are those who think that their narrow, stupid little world *is* the real universe, and who feel there is nothing more to be learned about it.

According, then, to Moskvitin – and Husserl – man finds himself in a most peculiar situation. He believes that he is in a 'real' world which encloses him and limits his freedom, so that for most of his life, his role is merely that of an observer. He feels essentially *passive*. This, says Mokvitin, is untrue. This world that we take for real is projected from some creative centre inside us, and our so called 'observation' is, in fact, a continuous act of creative transformation. He compares the process of perception to the scanning mechanism of a television set, and says that it is as if objects were 'licked' with a tongue. He goes on:

'Now let us imagine that we ourselves were able to look into this process. . . . Let us suppose that we were suddenly permitted to see the world external to us "as we see it". Imagine that step by step we are withdrawing our attention. . . . The first thing we should notice is that the world is not homogeneous and continuous; on the contrary, the projection of the retina will make the whole picture more like a mosaic, something like a painting by Seurat or Van Gogh. At the next point, when we focus attention on the firing of the impulse reactions, we should instead see the mosaic dissolving or continually fluctuating as if the whole thing were composed of myriads of small dancing sparks or mad molecules. A next step would be to see the spikes themselves – the transmission of the impulses down the channels. We should then see the sparks with traces or long tails after them. . . .'

Out of this insight would arise the realization that the external world is, in a sense, created by the power of this inner magician. Man does not understand his own power, so he remains little better than a worm, unaware of the astonishing secrets of the transcendental ego. Camus's *L'Étranger* paints an accurate picture of how most of us see ourselves: as little more than mirrors, passively reflecting reality. We may, like Meursault, be quite happy about that reality. But if we become nervous or depressed, this cheerful acceptance quickly turns into a sense of 'absurdity', of being trapped in the repetitive meaninglessness of the world. Yet this, in itself, is an absurdity. It is as if a theatrical designer who had been painting the scenery for the prison in Beethoven's *Fidelio* had a lapse of memory, and became convinced that he was locked up in prison. Roquentin, the hero of Sartre's *Nausea*, feels that reality is so real that it completely negates the human mind. He believes that we can only treat reality so cavalierly because we never stop to question the absurd ideas we impose on it – rather like some busybody in a comedy who mistakes a marquis for a servant, and gives him orders, which the marquis, out of amusement and sheer good nature, obeys. Sartre's attitude is only possible because it *is* true that we have separated ourselves from our intuitive faculties. Living in the left brain means that we are in a permanent state of 'forgetfulness'. So it is easy for this forgetfulness to go one stage further, and become nervous and self-effacing. It is as if the busybody realized suddenly that the marquis is not a footman, and allows the shock to scatter his wits and completely undermine his belief that anything is what it appears to be.

According to Moskvitin, all visionaries have glimpsed the basic mechanism of the 'sparks', and so come to realize intuitively that the inner self is a magician. He cites E.T.A. Hoffmann's story 'The Golden Pot', in which the hero has a vision of golden snakes twining themselves in the branches of an elderberry bush and moving so fast that it is as if the bush 'was spreading a thousand sparkling emeralds among its leaves'. He also quotes Isak Dinesen's unfinished story 'The Caryatids', a grim little drama about incest. The sister, who is unknowingly married to her half-brother, goes to consult a gypsy, and is shown a vision in the mill pond. It consists of 'a pattern of glowing red sparks', which becomes a red evening sky. 'The sparks were not a pattern on a dark ground, they were themselves the background.' Dinesen uses the interesting phrase: 'all at once, the noise around her changed; it had sense; it spoke'. This is, of course, the essence of the visionary experience: that sudden sense of deep significance. And the girl feels 'a deep ecstasy about this new world opened to her'.

Why deep ecstasy? There is nothing in her vision actually to cause ecstasy. The ecstasy of visionary states springs from a glimpse of the mechanism of 'vision', the recognition that its source is the 'inner magician'. We can observe the same thing in the famous passage in Proust, in which the narrator tastes the cake dipped in tea, and is suddenly carried back to his childhood. 'I had ceased to feel mediocre, accidental, mortal.' But why should this sudden clear memory of childhood produce a feeling of ecstasy? We are all capable of answering that question, for we have all experienced similar 'glimpses' of the past: a smell of Blackpool rock brings back days at the seaside, a smell of hot loaves from a bakery suddenly conjures up the bakery we passed on the way home from school at the age of seven. . . . The smell triggers a sense of freedom. Freedom from what? From our sense of being trapped in the present, like a fly stuck on fly paper, from the belief that we are the slaves of matter. The prophecies of Blake are full of attempts to express this sense of entrapment. Los, the creative principle – the 'divine imagination' – is bound in deadly sleep:

And now his eternal life
Like a dream was obliterated.

And in *Visions of the Daughters of Albion*:

They told me that the day and night were all that I could see;
They told me that I had five senses to inclose me up,
And they inclosed my infinite brain into narrow circle,

And sunk my heart into the abyss, a red, round globe, hot
   burning,
Till all from life I was obliterated and erased.
Instead of morn arises a bright shadow, like an eye
In the eastern cloud; instead of night a sickly charnel house . . .'

In *Europe*, the female principle declares:

Go! tell the human race that woman's love is sin;
That an eternal life awaits the worm of sixty winters
In an allegorical abode where existence hath never come. . . .

In poem after poem, Blake finds symbols to express the way
that the spirit somehow becomes blinded and falls into a state of
amnesia. The culprit seems to be Reason, symbolized as the god
Urizen: that is to say, the left brain. And again and again, man
falls into this state of amnesia from what appears to be a pleasant
and promising condition. In *Europe*, Los is just celebrating a vic-
tory over the forces of repression and stupidity, and his wife,
Enitharmon, feels that it is now time for peace and comfort and
relaxation. And this desire for comfortable domesticity allows
mankind to slip into a state of amnesia and delusion, so that man
comes to believe he is a mere 'worm of sixty winters'. (Blake
seems to be attacking the Christian church, which he identifies
with priestcraft and repression.) Finally, the spirit of revolution
awakens in France, and Los 'called all his sons to the strife of
blood'. Blake feels, like Yeats, that

When a man is fighting mad
Something drops from eyes long blind
He completes his partial mind. . . .

These glimpses of joy and power are the key to man's inner
possibilities. But it would be a mistake to think of them as semi-
mystical experiences. They are as familiar as eating and drinking.
We all experience them thousands of times in the course of a lifetime. Setting out on a holiday, or simply setting out for the office
on a sunny morning, something inside us wakes up, and there is a

curious tingle of sheer joy, of 'absurd good news'. Some power seems to stir inside us, and awakens a hunger which is in some ways like physical hunger. In our usual state of consciousness, new experience is, on the whole, rejected as an interruption. The telephone rings as we are settling down with the evening newspaper, and we curse irritably. A child, full of the appetite for new experience, rushes eagerly to answer the door or the telephone; he is full of an 'expectancy' that the adult has rejected.

According to Moskvitin, there is another way to achieve the glimpses of joy and power: to make deliberate use of dreams and hallucinations. This is because he believes that the 'inner magician' who shapes our perceptions can be seen directly at work in dreams. This certainly seems to be confirmed, for example, by those who have taken opium. In March 1804, Thomas De Quincey, at the age of nineteen, was suffering from rheumatic pains in his head and face, as a result of falling asleep with wet hair. He bought a bottle of tincture of opium from a druggist in Oxford Street, and gulped down the prescribed quantity as soon as he was back in his lodgings. '. . . and in an hour, O heavens! . . . what a resurrection, from its lowest depths, of the inner spirit! what an apocalypse of the world within me! . . . here was the secret of happiness, about which philosophers had disputed for so many ages.'

De Quincey insists that the effect of opium is a sense of clarity and power, not a descent into some warm and muddled dream world. 'The Opium Eater . . . feels that the diviner part of his nature is paramount – that is, the moral affections are in a state of cloudless serenity, and high over all the great light of the majestic intellect.' He speaks of 'the abyss of divine enjoyment', of the power of opium to build 'out of the fantastic imagery of the brain, cities and temples, beyond the art of Phidias and Praxiteles, beyond the splendour of Babylon and Hecatombpylos'.

It seems, then, that the chief quality of opium was to free De Quincey from his sense of being a victim of material reality. On the page before he takes the drug, his account remarks: 'It was a Sunday afternoon, wet and cheerless; and a duller spectacle this earth of ours has not to show than a rainy Sunday in London.' We all know the feeling – as if the spirit is being dragged downward by some enormous force of gravity that makes us feel weak and helpless. Opium restored a sense of power, of *control*. And part of this control was the ability to create magnificent scenes inside his head. Which suggests that the sense of joy and power created by opium is not purely a physical effect, like the sense of well-being experienced by a hungry man when he eats a hot meal. It is a 'glimpse', like the 'exquisite pleasure' Proust describes on tasting the cake dipped in herb tea. Blake would have said it is a glimpse of the powers of the soul, of the Divine Imagination.

De Quincey himself recognized this to be true. In the *Opium Eater* he describes a visit to the opera under the influence of opium, and how deeply he enjoyed the music. 'The mistake of most people is to suppose that it is by the ear they communicate with music. But this is not so; it is by the reaction of the mind upon the notices of the ear, (the *matter* coming from the senses, the *form* from the mind) that the pleasure is constructed. . . . Now opium by greatly increasing the activity of the mind generally, increases, of necessity, that particular mode of its activity by which we are able to construct out of the raw material of organic sound an elaborate intellectual pleasure.'

And this passage also clarifies a point that Moskvitin leaves in obscurity: what the inner magician *does* to the reality of the external world. The music De Quincey was listening to had already been written; the mind of the composer had already stamped it with meaning. So the opium did not transform the music into some celestial melody; it merely increased De Quincey's power to grasp the reality of the music. And the sense of joy and tranquillity induced by opium springs from the mind's *increased grasp* of the reality outside us. Moskvitin's achievement is in making it so clear that we grasp reality in a rather complicated way, which is analogous to a television camera translating points of light into electrical impulses, which are then fired from a kind of gun and transplanted back into points of light on the television screen.

It is easy to make the mistake of assuming that the television screen on which we see 'the world' is a mirror faithfully reflecting what is in front of it. This mistake gives rise to the 'passive fallacy', the feeling that reality *is* what it is and that there is nothing much we can do about it. This is what Meursault feels as he looks out of his window on a Sunday afternoon; it is also what De Quincey felt in Oxford Street. Reality is 'a bore'. So the spirit droops and yawns. Opium revealed to De Quincey what his flash of rage revealed to Meursault: that a burst of energy can *alter the senses*, so the world suddenly becomes 'rich and strange'. The inner magician can alter the quality of the picture, just as the television controls enable us to heighten the colour or increase the definition.

This is a question that must be explored more fully in the final chapter. Meanwhile, let us return to the question of the nature of the 'inner vision' induced by opium or psychedelic drugs – or, in Brad's case, simply by deep relaxation. We observe that De Quincey talks about magnificent palaces and statues – he felt that a granite statue of Rameses II in the British Museum symbolized the serenity and strength of the mind in opium reverie – but not about the usual coloured patterns that have become familiar to us from the psychedelic literature. Coleridge also took opium, and he had visions that sound rather more like the results of mescalin or LSD – a spectrum with a pattern like a pheasant's tail, and vivid kaleidoscopes of colours. He spoke 'of figures, even with open eyes, of squares . . . and of various colours.' In her book *Opium and the Romantic Imagination*, Alethea Hayter remarks that 'opium by strengthening the combining power and heightening the emotion, has already brought these dreams halfway to conscious literary creation'. This certainly seems to have happened in the case of De Quincey's weirdly complicated dreams – described in *Suspiria de Profundis* and *The English Mail Coach*, or of Coleridge's *Kubla Khan*. So the effects of opium seem to be strangely complex, ranging from simple patterns to curious inner voyages, such as the one described in Brad's 'Old man' poem. The common-sense view is that drugs plunge the mind into a completely irrational world of nightmare, and that it would be futile to subject these visions to rational analysis. Yet De Quincey and Coleridge plainly feel otherwise. And Moskvitin's theory provides a rationale. He would say that the tremendous selective and creative power of the inner magician is given free rein by the drug, but moulded by the dreamer's memory in the way that ordinary physical perception is moulded by our expectations of the external world. By a fortunate accident, Brad was able to release some of these powers without the use of drugs, and the inner magician made him aware of its presence by demonstrating the range of its creativity.

Why did it express itself in patterns rather than in 'visionary' paintings, like those of Blake or Van Gogh? Here Moskvitin offers a clue. If the mechanisms of perception are analogous to the mechanisms of a television screen, then perception breaks down into 'units' of patterns. Look at a newspaper photograph; perhaps it shows a wedding, or a statesman climbing on to an aeroplane. There are no obvious patterns. Now look at it through a magnifying glass, and you see that it is actually a grid of dots, and that it consists entirely of patterns. A close look at a television screen showing a videotape reveals the same thing; at close quarters, the texture of the picture resembles a piece of cloth, with a warp and woof. And again, we become aware of patterns. Look at the scenery as you drive along in a car. At first you are only aware of *things* – trees, fences, clouds, fields, houses. But now look at them with a painter's eye, or as if you were looking at a series of colour photographs. You now become aware of 'compositions' – colours and shapes blending in various ways. Your visual field is made up of patterns. But if you were a photographer or a painter, you would reject most of these 'compositions' because they lack harmony. That gasworks spoils the composition; that cloud should be in the middle; that overhanging branch of the tree should be on the other side. . . . But the inner magician has no such problems. He can choose harmony in every composition. Brad has described how, as his hand reached out for a certain colour, he thought: 'Oh no, that can't be right.' But it always was.

In short, if the inner magician chooses to display his versatility as a painter, what is more natural than that he should work in coloured patterns?

5
From Negative to Positive Freedom

During those last four or five days at Viittakivi, I spent as much time as possible with Brad. My meeting with him struck me as an astonishing piece of Jungian synchronicity, and I felt I would be a fool not to take advantage of it. The stresses of the six months before I left England had convinced me that the answers to some of our major problems lie in the right cerebral hemisphere. I had come to Viittakivi with the intention of trying to teach a discipline based upon this recognition. And in Viittakivi I had met a man who seemed to be the perfect illustration of my theories. Yet there was still a great deal I wanted to know. Important discoveries are seldom made without some kind of preparation. In Brad's case, I felt intuitively that the story had begun long before the traumatic experience with his adopted son. So with the tape recorder switched on, I asked him to give me an account of his life before he came to Finland.

Ronald Bradley Absetz was born in Buffalo, New York, on 10 March 1928. (I thought: of course, a Pisces: the romantic dreamer.) And he was twenty-two before he began to suspect that his unconscious had, so to speak, a mind of its own.

It was during the summer vacation of 1950, when he was a student at Oberlin College. He had decided to spend the summer in the Bay area of California, working in a fruit cannery.

On his first day in Oakland, he found himself a room, paid a month's rent, bought a supply of food, and spent the evening reading the situation-vacant ads in the local newspapers. He marked several possible jobs, and prepared to go and find work

83

early the next morning. But when he woke up, he felt sleepy and lethargic, and decided to stay in bed. He spent most of the day in bed, and got up in the late afternoon, in time to buy milk and bread, and the evening newspapers. Again, he read the situation-vacant ads and marked those that looked promising. The next morning, he felt the same reluctance to get out of bed. Assuming that the hitch-hike from Ohio to California had tired him more than he realized, he decided to spend the day in his room again. But when the same thing happened for the rest of the week, he began to feel a mixture of irritation and bewilderment. By evening, he could usually work up the energy to go out and buy food and newspapers; but when he woke up the next morning, he felt will-less and purposeless. In his third week, he travelled to the next town, where his mother lived, to borrow money. He told her only that he was still looking for work. And so the paralysis of the will to act continued for another three weeks. During the day he wanted only to lie in bed and doze; everything seemed too much effort. By evening he had worked up the energy to go out; but it had evaporated by the next morning.

One day, he remembered that he had promised to prepare a bulletin for in-coming college freshmen back at Oberlin. A sense of guilt forced him to go out and buy wax stencils, and to spend that evening typing the bulletin. This effort seemed to break the strange inner paralysis. The next morning, he went to the post office to send it off, then went on to a fruit cannery and got a job. And for the rest of the vacation he worked strenuously; the mysterious lethargy was forgotten.

Back at Oberlin in the autumn, he threw himself back into his studies, and into various extra-curricular activities. As a student, Brad was noted for his seriousness and enthusiasm – this is what made the period of lethargy so incomprehensible. Finally, it struck him that he had made no effort to try to understand what had happened, and he decided to consult the student counsellor. Her name was Frances Seaman, and she was a friend and admirer of the 'existential psychologist' Carl Rogers. She was convinced that most people have the capacity to grow and develop according to certain inner laws, and that her business was to try to help that growth to happen. It was a good relationship, and Brad found it helpful. They often spent most of the therapeutic session sitting in silence – she seemed to believe naturally in 'relaxing into the right brain'. And one day, as they sat in silence, Brad had an experience that sounds like Jung's 'active imagination'. As if in a 'clear, strong dream', he saw himself beside a well, carrying a case full of tools. As he put down the case on the ground, looking into the well, he saw a baby lying in the bottom of the well. There was no need for him to interpret the 'dream'; he already knew what it meant. 'The baby was my inner self who had been born at the same time as my outer physical self, but had been kept down at the bottom of the well; that all the tools of analysis and understanding in that case on the ground had served . . . to bring me to this well and discover this infant form of my inner person – and that these tools were no longer necessary. What was necessary was that I should lift the baby from that deep well and allow it to develop and grow.' The baby, he felt, was trying to express itself through his adult body. What absurd and embarrassing things could happen to an infant 'inner self' in an adult body? The thought threw him into a panic in which he was afraid that he was going to disintegrate. Gradually, the panic subsided as he realized that he was still in one piece – mentally as well as physically. This 'vision' convinced him that the therapy had served its purpose and could be discontinued.

When Brad told me this story, he seemed apologetic, as if unsure whether he was wasting my time; when he finished, he sat in silence for a while, then asked: 'I don't know if that helps?' It did indeed – far more than he could possibly realize. Suddenly, in a flash of excitement and insight, I saw the whole pattern. All the other things he had told me now fitted together.

Brad's parents had imbued him with the Protestant work ethic. They were alone in a strange country – his father's parents were Slovaks from the Austro-Hungarian empire, and Brad's family were the only people called Absetz in the whole United States. Salvation lay in hard work and high moral standards. Brad and his brother were taught to be good Christians – which meant continual involvement in church activities – and to behave 'like gentlemen'. His father was unemployed through most of the 1930s, so the need to preserve standards seemed even greater. At school, a slight speech defect led to much teasing – his 's's sounded like 'sh', so that 'sit' came out as 'shit'. Speech therapy eliminated the defect, but the shyness and loneliness remained.

At the age of seventeen he enlisted for two years in the US Navy. At the training station in San Diego he realized 'that no one there would know me – that any kind of person I chose to be would be considered "he who naturally is" by everyone. This insight coincided with a need I had noticed growing in myself – a need to change, to become something more/or/else than I had been up to that time.' He decided to call himself by his middle name, Brad, instead of Ron. When he came out of the navy, he was able to continue his education at the government's expense, and decided on Oberlin because it was one of the smallest colleges in the United States, with a student–teacher ratio of fifteen to one (compared to about a hundred to one at the University of California.) He felt that he needed a 'supportive' environment to allow his personality to develop naturally. He experienced an instinctive revulsion for 'the rat race'. And then, in his second year at college, he set out to spend the summer vaction in Oakland, California. . . .

The 'waking dream' of the baby in the well is another example of the ability of Brad's unconscious mind to solve problems when given the opportunity to express itself. Gurdjieff made an important distinction between 'essence' and 'personality'. Personality is the outer self, the part that has learned to cope with other people and with the world. Essence is the inner being, and in most of us, its development lags far behind that of the personality. Personality reacts mechanically to events and circumstances. Under stress, it tends to bend or break. Essence is the part of us that enables us to stand alone, to make our own decisions, if necessary to ignore the opinions of other people and swim against the tide. Shy people are particularly prone to leave their essence undeveloped, because their biggest problem is to learn to blend with the crowd, to feel themselves a part of society. They often spend so much effort on developing protective coloration that they have no energy left for deciding what they really want out of life.

Brad's early training – the Protestant work ethic, the insistence on behaving 'like a gentleman' – provided the protective coloration. At school he was a typical 'outsider', with his speech defect and his naturally shy and introverted temperament. At sixteen he had his first opportunity to develop a more positive 'self-image' when he went to live with his maternal grandmother in Canada. Then came the navy, and a new self-confidence; Ron Absetz became Brad. At Oberlin he joined a church group, and threw himself into voluntary and social activities. The self-image – the personality – was developing nicely.

The trouble with personality is that its motivation needs to come from outside. It reacts to people, to situations, to external stimuli. Like a donkey, it needs carrots to make it break into a gallop. Which explains what happened in Oakland. Alone in a room, with no one else looking on, no one to please or impress, Brad found his mainspring was no longer there.

Machado de Assis has a story called 'The Looking Glass' that expresses the problem with great clarity and precision. A young man from a small village joins the army and becomes a lieutenant. When he comes home in his uniform, everyone admires him. An aunt who owns a remote farm presses him to come and stay; she orders the servants to address him as '*Signor lieutenant*'. But both the aunt and uncle are unexpectedly called away to sick relatives, and the slaves on the farm take the opportunity to desert. The young soldier is left totally alone. As the days go by he experiences a sense of emptiness and meaninglessness; his personality seems to be dissolving. In the large mirror in his bedroom, even his own reflection seems blurred. Then he has an idea. He takes his uniform out of its chest, and puts it on. Then he walks up and down in front of the mirror. Suddenly, he feels 'real' again. And he does this daily until his aunt and uncle return. . . .

Machado begins his story by saying that man has two souls, one outside and looking in, one inside and looking out. He means, of course, essence and personality. Like Brad at the age of twenty-two, the young lieutenant has a baby inside him looking out.

The act of forcing himself to type the bulletin set in motion the wheels of Brad's personality; it was the equivalent of putting on his uniform and standing in front of a mirror. He once again allowed his conduct to be dictated by what was expected of him. And so the experience of '*accidia*' – the word Christian ascetics used for these periods of inner deadness – came to an end. Most people would have been glad to forget the experience, or write it off as some form of exhaustion. Brad seems to have recognized that there was more to it than that.

And in fact, the problem returned two years later. During his senior years at Oberlin, Brad became involved in the student cooperative movement. The students rented two dormitories from the college and operated them on a basis of shared responsibilities. The North American Students' Cooperative League was persuaded to move its offices to Oberlin, where it could be run by the students' cooperative. Brad agreed to serve as coordinator, with the task of forging links between students' cooperatives throughout the US and Canada. In effect, it became a one-man operation with Brad in charge. In December 1953 and January 1954 he toured campuses throughout the US and Canada, making ambitious plans.

On his return to Oberlin, he rested for a couple of days before settling down to work. And once again, the relaxation turned into lethargy, paralysis of the ability to act. 'This time I felt that the message was clear: there was something about the job, as exciting and challenging as it seemed, that unconscious levels in me were forcefully rejecting. . . .' And after two more months of lethargy, he felt there was no alternative to resignation. This was something of a disaster for the student cooperative organization, since Brad had become its mainspring. The decision to abandon the path of 'duty' must have involved a great deal of guilt and self-reproach. But the *accidia* seemed to leave no alternative.

And so for a second time Brad obeyed the dictates of an obscure, unconscious urge, which had given a sign that he needed a change of direction. He had failed to obtain his degree, having less than the required number of marks in French; he was advised to stay on for another year and re-take the French examination. Instead, he left the relative comfort and security of the college, and took a job on a freighter as assistant cook. In the September of 1954, he sailed for Europe; his only prospective income was of periodic payments from someone who had bought his motor bike. When this failed to materialize, he had to think urgently about employment. At the flat of a girl-friend in Paris, he saw a brochure about Viittakivi – the girl had vaguely intended to go, then changed her mind. Brad wrote to enquire about a scholarship and, to his delight, received in reply a friendly letter beginning 'Dear Brad'. The writer was a girl who had been a fellow student at Oberlin, and who was now teaching at Viittakivi. The coincidence was remarkable, since Oberlin has such a small student body. Even Brad's hitch-hiking trip to Finland seemed to reveal the same hand of providence. At the Dutch frontier, the guard refused to let him through since he had so little money. He turned back, intending to try another frontier crossing. The first car that came along picked him up; when he told the driver his destination, the driver said that his brother would be making the trip to Finland in two days' time, and could give Brad a lift.

This is how it came about that, in the January of 1955, Brad finally arrived in the country that he would come to accept as his home. 'My first impression of the far North – of snow-covered southern Sweden and Finland in January – was of almost endless open space on every side; with the few widely scattered farmhouses separated by vast stretches of snow-covered fields, rolling hills and ridges that were dotted with occasional hay sheds. I felt that we were travelling over a sparsely inhabited infinity plane. Viittakivi was also located in such solitude, with the spaciousness framed on two sides by the pine and spruce forests. . . .'

When the scholarship ran out, he became leader of an international work camp in Lapland, then replaced the fellow Oberlin student as a part-time teacher. When he was offered this job, he told the director, Elvi Saari, frankly about his experiences of *accidia*, and admitted that he could not guarantee that he would not succumb to another attack. She shrugged and said that it didn't matter; if it happened again, they might all learn something from it. 'That freedom to fail was one of the most important gifts anyone had ever given me.' And, understandably, the *accidia* never recurred.

So, in due course, Brad married a Finnish girl, became the father of three children, and eventually became a full-time teacher at Viittakivi, with a salary and paid holidays. He was now in his mid thirties, and it was the first time in his life that he experienced this kind of security. It looked as if the long search was over; he had found his 'supportive environment', and a job that offered the freedom for personal development. And it was at this point that his wife had a miscarriage, and they decided to adopt a mulatto baby. So just as he seemed to have achieved security, Brad was, in fact, entering upon the most painful and traumatic period of his life. The result was the 'movement impulses', the paintings and the poems.

With the benefit of hindsight, it is easy enough to see what happened. Since early childhood, Brad had been driven by the sense of obligation, of duty, that had been instilled by his parents. And the same external necessity had continued to be his main motivating force during his period in the navy and the first year at Oberlin. The right brain, the creative intuition, never had a chance to express itself. When he had paid the month's rent on the room in Oakland, external necessity was suddenly removed. He was 'free'. But free for what? This was a problem that faced many of his generation. Arthur Miller had written about it in *Death of a Salesman*, in the character of Biff Loman, the son who doesn't seem to want a regular job. Jack Kerouac had also written about it, in a novel called *On the Road* which, in 1955, had still not found a publisher. A whole generation – in Europe as well as America – was bored with the 'success ethic' and the conventional wisdom. Brad never became a drifter like Biff Loman, or a dharma bum like Kerouac; but something inside him insisted that modern American society and its values were not for him. That first 'breakdown' in Oakland was a confrontation with his own lack of a mainspring, the second occurred when he was revealing his organizational abilities in the students' cooperative. In all probability, he would have become its permanent organizer. And the 'other self' groaned with boredom at the prospect.

Yet even the 'supportive environment' of Viittakivi could provide no real solution. Again, it was the problem: freedom for what? The answer came only after the death of Kalevala, his adopted son, and his wife's schizophrenic breakdown. In the hours of silent, relaxed concentration, lying beside her, Brad's 'other self' at last succeeded in making its voice heard. And, for perhaps the first time in his life, Brad began to live and act 'from inside', instead of from external necessity.

Expressed in this way, the achievement sounds unimportant enough. But this is because we continue to judge these things in terms of conventional success. In 1957, publication of *On the Road* made Kerouac famous; it looked as if this younger generation of Americans had found a solution to the problem of Arthur Miller's salesman. Yet we know that, in a practical sense, Kerouac never found his solution; the biography by Anne Charters shows a man who is slowly losing control, drifting into breakdown and alcoholism. Timothy Leary advised his students to 'tune in and drop out', and a whole generation followed his advice and abandoned the rat-race to smoke pot and drop acid. The trial of the Manson family in 1969 made it obvious that the hippie ethic was open to great abuse and was not the solution Kerouac and Leary had been looking for.

The same criticism could be levelled at the post-war existentialist movement in Europe. This generation had the advantage of having known Nazi oppression at first hand; they understood the meaning of freedom. In August 1945, when the Germans were being driven out of Paris, Camus wrote an article in the underground newspaper *Combat* that began: 'Paris is shooting all her bullets in the August night. In this vast setting of stones and waters, all round this river that has reflected so much history, the barricades of freedom have once more been thrown up.' And he ended: 'This huge Paris . . . is bursting with all the fires of hope and suffering, it has the flame of lucid courage and all the glow, not only of liberation, but of tomorrow's liberty'. But the course of 'tomorrow's liberty' was charted by Simone de Beauvoir in her novel *The Mandarins*, which opens with the liberation of Paris, and in which both Camus and Sartre figure as central characters. Tomorrow's liberty has failed to materialize. They drink and smoke and talk all night in cellars in St Germain, they fornicate and change partners, they discuss politics – and boredom hangs over them like a faint odour of decay. The point is reinforced in Herbert Lottman's biography of Camus; he tells of a heavy night's drinking in St Germain, and how 'they continued their drinking in a bistro in the Halles neighbourhood, wept for humanity as they walked across a bridge over the Seine. "To think that in a few hours I'm going to talk about the writer's responsibility," Sartre remarked, referring to a lecture he was to give that day at the Sorbonne; Camus laughed.' In fact, Camus had been pitchforked into fame before he was ready for it. He was a simple, unaffected man who liked talking and drinking with friends. He was also an unashamed womanizer who found it practically impossible to be faithful to his wife. Such a way of life is hardly conducive to the 'mandarin' frame of mind. And the detailed portrait of Sartre that emerges from Simone de Beauvoir's autobiographies makes it clear that he suffered from the same problem. Gurdjieff would have said that essence lagged behind personality. Both were compelled to assume a mantle of intellectual seriousness that would have been loose even on Goethe or Tolstoy. Camus felt the strain more than Sartre – whose leftist affiliations made his isolation easier to bear – and when the Nobel Prize brought the inevitable backlash of denigration, it plunged him into a depression that brought him to the edge of nervous breakdown. The writing block had still not disappeared at the time of his pointless death in the car accident. Sartre lived on for another two decades, but the major work that was to have reconciled his existentialist philosophy and his Marxist politics – the *Critique of Dialectical Reason* – remained unfinished, a symbol of his inability to solve the dilemma.

The generation of writers that emerged in England in the mid 1950s – and which included myself – faced an analogous problem. The heroes of John Osborne, Kingsley Amis, John Wain, Iris Murdoch, John Braine, Arnold Wesker, showed the same anti-bourgeois tendency as the heroes of existentialism or the Beat Generation. They also wanted to find a way of life that was a spontaneous expression of the urge to freedom. On the whole, the revolt of the 'angry young men' was a matter of negative emotional attitudes. In attacking the British 'establishment', they had chosen an easy target; and the establishment reacted in its normal manner, listening sympathetically, and then slowly absorbing the rebels. My own work differed from that of the other 'angries' in being totally unconcerned with social issues; *The Outsider* was a study in the paradox of freedom: that, as Fichte says, to be free is nothing; to *become* free is heavenly. Its success was greater than anyone expected – it had been translated into twenty or so languages before the end of the decade – and convinced me for a short time that the problem of inner freedom is of interest to an enormous number of people. Critics described us as the representatives of a new generation, while one journalist denounced us as 'messiahs of the milk-bars'. It was interesting and exciting to be regarded as 'intellectual leaders', and to join in discussions on the writer's responsibility in *Encounter* and *Les Temps Modernes*. But I think that most of us had the same sense of incongruity that Sartre and Camus experienced as they walked back from their night's drinking. And it soon became clear to me that there was no enormous audience waiting to join in the discussion about human freedom; in England there is not even a small audience. (Probably the situation was the same in France, but disguised by the success of 'existentialist' catchwords.) At all events, as I watched the angry young men turn into successful middle-aged men, I could see clearly that this problem could only be solved on the individual and personal level; political revolt is irrelevant. Both Camus and Sartre had been neatly hog-tied by their earlier radicalism. Camus came to see that rebellion is a political roundabout that revolves back into the same old tyranny; too ashamed to admit that he had outgrown his leftism, he found himself in an intellectual cul-de-sac. Sartre accused Camus of being a reactionary; but he paid for his own refusal to re-examine his political convictions by congealing into a grotesque attitude of permanent indignation, shaking his fist at some abstract

Authority. Where politics was concerned, he seemed determined to be guided by his emotions.

The point I am making should be clear. Nothing is plainer, more simple, more direct, than the *impulse* to freedom. And nothing is simpler than taking the first step, which consists of rejection: of conventional ties, of the bourgeoisie, of the establishment. But this only produces negative freedom, of the kind Fichte meant when he said: 'To be free is nothing.' Most rebellions end here. The rebel knows clearly what he *doesn't* want; but he is less sure about what he wants. Some feel that since this is a 'spiritual' problem, the answer should be sought in religion. But there is no evidence that various twentieth-century writers who accepted this solution – Chesterton, Eliot, Greene, Waugh, Lewis – have found it a source of positive freedom. Thomas Merton, who followed his impulse of retreat to its logical conclusion – behind the walls of a Trappist monastery – seems to have been more frustrated as a monk than he was as a layman. The problem was still waiting for him in his cell.

When Brad experienced the paralysis of will in Oakland, he had taken the step into negative freedom. He retreated into the security of university life, but repeated the rejection process when he threw up the post of secretary of the student's cooperative. The trip to Europe was an attempt to find out what to do next. But his arrival at Viittakivi was no solution. Admittedly, Viittakivi had become a centre for people involved in the same search; most of those who go there feel that modern civilization has taken the wrong turning, and that life must somehow recover its individual dimension. But although the existence of places like Viittakivi guarantees a forum for discussion of the problem, it can no more provide solutions than can a Trappist monastery. It was Brad's recognition of this fact that led him to leave Viittakivi after his marriage, and to plan to move to India. The arrival of a family made this impracticable, and it is difficult not to feel that he would have found it ultimately unsatisfying – Brad was in search of an ideal, not of a country. He returned to Viittakivi as a full-time instructor. And the ordeal of the death of his adopted son and the illness of his wife finally revealed the solution, and provided the step into positive freedom. In those hours of inner suspension, lying beside his wife, simultaneously attentive and relaxed, that 'other self' found that its voice could be heard, and that it would no longer be ignored or overruled by the practical ego. Brad had, in fact, taken a vital step towards solving a problem that has preoccupied artists, philosophers and poets for almost two centuries.

6
A Century of Misunderstanding

Let us, at this point, look back at the nature of that problem.

It is, as Moskvitin recognized, the problem of 'visionary consciousness', of states of mind in which we become aware of what Wordsworth called 'unknown modes of being'. No doubt men have always longed for these states of visionary consciousness, and some of the saints have achieved them. But where European literature is concerned, they appear for the first time in the writings of the romantics, in the poetry of Wordsworth, Blake and Novalis, the fiction of Jean Paul Richter and E.T.A. Hoffmann. (Moskvitin points out that Hoffman's vision of green snakes seems to be a glimpse of the actual mechanism of this vision.)

In its most basic form, it is simply a feeling of excitement, of happiness and affirmation. This is accompanied by an insight that seems to be purely objective: that reality is infinitely deeper and richer than it appears to ordinary perception: that, in some paradoxical sense, everyday consciousness is a liar. Early romantics tried to capture the feeling in images of sensual bliss; this is Novalis, from *Heinrich von Ofterdingen*:

'He approached the basin, which surged and quivered in endless colours. This fluid, which was not hot but cool, covered the walls of the cave, where it emitted only a faint bluish light. He dipped his hand into the basin and wet his lips. It was as though a spirit breathed through him, and he felt deeply refreshed and strengthened. An irresistible longing to bathe seized him; he undressed and stepped down into the basin. It seemed as if a sunset cloud was enveloping him; a heavenly sensation flowed through his soul; with voluptuous delight countless thoughts strove to mingle within him. New images never seen before arose and interfused and became visible around him, and every wave of the lovely element clung to him like a tender blossom. The waves appeared to be charming girls dissolved, which momentarily embodied themselves as they touched the youth.'

'It was as if a spirit breathed through him. . . .' The sexual imagery of the final sentence is not accidental; the romantics associated this 'heavenly sensation' with sexual bliss, the delight of feeling a girl's naked body against one's bare skin. The romantic ecstasy has much in common with sexual ecstasy. In these moments, it is natural for us to compare the sensation to a surge of electric current that causes a bulb to glow twice as brightly. The romantic was inclined to compare it to the wind. In *The Prophet*, Pushkin likens the poet's heart to a live coal; but a coal has to wait for the wind to make it glow. The force of Shelley's 'Ode to the west wind' springs from our recognition that he is really speaking about this vital current:

> Make me thy lyre, even as the forest is. . . .

In 'Winter', Pushkin describes the far more common sensation of the poet's sense of helplessness when the wind fails to blow:

> Slow drop by drop I drink my boredom's bitter poison.
> I try a book; the eyes glide down the page – in vain.
> My thoughts are far away. . . .

This is the problem that discouraged the romantics: that there is no infallible method of 'raising the wind', of controlling the current. Yet in Pushkin, we can observe that the problem is, to some extent, self-created. Like a spoilt child, he feels that life has no right to bore him – how dare it make him swallow this nasty medicine? And the next line of Shelley's poem – 'What if my leaves are falling like its own!' – betrays the same note of self-pity. The romantics in general were inclined to raise indignant wails of reproach, like a child complaining that its soup is half-cold. Proust explains smugly that he has always been subject to nervous debility, and is liable to suffer agonies of migraine and insomnia if he drinks tea too late at night. . . . Yet in his vast autobiographical novel, Proust came closer than any of the romantics to gripping the problem of 'vision' in the forceps of analysis. He recognized the essentially paradoxical nature of the experience: how we can be feeling bored and listless one moment, and then quite suddenly experience a momentary immortality, a sense of power, of insight, of vision. What is more, we are not swept into these moments on the crest of a wave of ecstasy or vitality; they are only a hair's breadth away from the experience of fatigue and boredom. As Proust stands outside the public lavatory in the Champs-Élysées, waiting for his chaperone, he observes that 'the old damp walls of the entrance . . . emitted a cool, fusty smell which . . . filled me with a pleasure of a different kind from other pleasures, which leave one more unstable, incapable of grasping them, of possessing them, a pleasure that was solid and consistent, on which I could lean for support, delicious, soothing, rich with a truth that was lasting, unexplained and sure. I should have liked . . . to endeavour to penetrate the charm of this impression which had seized hold of me, and remaining there motionless, to explore this antiquated emanation which invited me not to enjoy the pleasure which it was offering me only as a bonus, but to descend into the underlying reality which it had not yet disclosed to me.' Proust recognizes that his normal grasp of reality is somehow false, and that moments like this bring a glimpse of another mode of understanding. This is what is so exciting in Proust, in spite of the hypochondria and self-indulgence: his recognition that this 'other reality' is *so close*. This is quite unlike the exquisite self-pity of Shelley's:

> Life, like a dome of many-coloured glass,
> Stains the white radiance of Eternity, . . .

with its implication that we would all be better off if we could escape this 'dim vast vale of tears'. Proust can somehow see that ordinary, everyday life could become a continuous delight if we could learn that trick of looking at things from a slightly different angle.

We now know something that Proust was in no position to know: that the change of angle is simply a movement of a couple of inches from one side of the brain to the other. (And I must emphasize that doubts about split-brain theory make no difference whatever; the difference between the 'two selves' *does* exist, whether or not they can be closely identified with the left and right.) All that has happened as he breathes in the smell of damp and fungus is that he is suddenly perceiving it *directly*, with 'primal perception', and not – as T.E. Lawrence says – filtered through and made typical by thought. As a hypochondriac, Proust was always creating false problems and tensions, working himself up into states of anxiety based on self-doubt – that is, the ego's sense of its own inadequacy. These 'glimpses' that came through smells and tastes – or even from stumbling on a cracked paving stone – were 'intimations of immortality' that by-passed the 'false self'. This becomes clear in the paving stone episode in the final volume, where Proust's narrator again experiences the 'all is well' feeling as he is momentarily transported back to St Mark's in Venice. He remarks that his doubts about his literary gift suddenly vanished 'as if by magic': 'I had followed no new train of reasoning, discovered no decisive argument, but the difficulties which had seemed insoluble a moment ago had lost all importance.' That slight change of angle has made them evaporate: and Proust recognizes that he has by-passed chains of reasoning and arguments – left-brain activities – for some form of direct perception.

These are not matter of 'mysticism' or poetics, but a central – perhaps *the* central – problem of philosophy. The problem is this. Reason seems to lead us to the truth about the world. The dialogues of Socrates are a series of demonstrations of how reason can lead to truth. Yet when we try to grasp the world by reason, we find ourselves involved in all kinds of problems and contradictions, and the truth seems further away than ever. Plato suggested what is happening in his myth of the cave – that human beings were like prisoners chained in a cave, seeing only the shadows cast by a fire on the wall and mistaking them for reality. If they could be unchained and allowed outside, they would be staggered by the real world. . . . But, thought Plato, reason can reveal this 'real world' to us – we only have to be educated to use our minds instead of living 'by rule of thumb'.

This belief of Plato was to cause much agony to later philosophers (for, as Whitehead remarked, western philosophy is little more than a series of footnotes to Plato). We can see why if we think of Proust's experience with the madeleine or the broken paving stone. These brought that sudden flash of direct insight, quite simply *a sense of reality* – like the prisoner released from the cave. Yet reason obviously played no part in the process. The more we reason, the more we seem to become entangled on our own logic. Dostoevsky experienced the 'sense of reality' when he was reprieved in front of a firing squad; what had that to do with reason? Yet to reject reason is no answer either; we only have to turn to Plato's dialogues to *see* that reason is precisely what he claimed – the most reliable gateway to truth.

From Descartes onward, modern philosophy has found itself in an apparently insoluble dilemma. Descartes believed that it should be possible to create a philosophy that should be as reliable as geometry or mathematics, and simply by subjecting everything to the test of reason – that is, of doubt. And he found it difficult to get beyond the basic proposition, 'I think therefore I am.' What if God is a conjuror, and the universe is a box of conjuring tricks, intended to deceive us? How could we tell? Hume pointed out that even the connection between cause and effect could be a conjuring trick. If the conjuror, for example, made water-falls go up instead of down, we would assume that to be 'natural' and inevitable. Berkeley went on to argue that, when considered from this strictly rational point of view, the real world can be doubted out of existence. And indeed, if the game is played according to the rules of left-brain logic, Berkeley and Hume are irrefutable. 'Sceptical logic', logic where everything has to be 'proved', can be compared to one of those mathematical games where you have to join up a number of dots without lifting the pencil from the paper or retracing any

line. What could be sillier than saying, 'I think, therefore I am'?
I am just as aware that 'I am' when I lie in bed, perfectly
contented and unthinking, a few moments after waking up,
or when I am involved in some emergency that forces me to
act without thinking; in fact, even more so. Doctor Johnson
went straight to the point when he tried to refute Berkeley by
kicking a stone; he was demonstrating that, where the business of experience is concerned, reason is the least important
of our faculties. In effect, we see the world simultaneously
through two pairs of eyes, one belonging to reason, the other
to intuition.

Kant instinctively recognized that this was the solution to
the problem; his 'Copernican revolution' amounts to grasping
that our minds *add* something to what we experience, so the
rationalist method of interrogating reality – as if what our senses
tell us is the whole truth and nothing but – is based upon a
fallacy. It is rather as if a detective interrogating a suspect should
suddenly realize that he is subject to hallucinations and 'voices',
so that half the testimony may be his own invention. Kant
recognized that our senses are 'active'. They do not 'contemplate' reality; they play their part in creating it. The 'you' who
looks at a clock to tell the time is not the *whole* you, but merely a
partial self, a left-brain façade; and if you try to construct a
philosophy on the testimony of this self, you will find yourself
involved in some baffling contradictions. Experience happens to
you; but you also happen to experience.

So when Camus's Meursault looks out of the window and
feels that life is 'absurd', or when Sartre's Roquentin decides
that the truth about reality is glimpsed in flashes of 'nausea',
they are falling into the same trap as Hume and Descartes. They
have not reached their conclusions through a process of philosophical argument, but by a kind of immediate perception: that
is, by a left-brain interpretation of direct experience. All true
philosophy – no matter how abstract and complex it sounds on
paper – has this foundation in the philosopher's immediate
experience of his own life. The fact that a perception – like
'nausea' – is immediate and powerful does not mean that it is
true.

'Nausea' is one of the commoner human experiences. It happens to us, in a mild form, every time we become tired or discouraged, and feel 'mediocre, accidental, mortal'. And nausea is only possible because we are capable of 'taking stock' of our situation. If you play a game with an insect, blocking its path with a twig, it never seems to become discouraged; it will continue indefatigably trying to find an unblocked path until it collapses with exhaustion. A man becomes discouraged long before because he 'contemplates' his situation; he may even get discouraged before he starts. The purpose of this faculty – of taking stock – is to enable us not to waste vital energy. But in practice, it causes us to waste a great deal. We exaggerate; we become over-excited; we succumb to anxiety and self-pity. In short, the rational ego loses touch with its intuitive partner. They could be compared to a married couple who go for a picnic; but the husband is so impatient and preoccupied that he walks on ahead until they have lost sight of one another. Unfortunately, the wife is carrying the bag with the food; so the husband starves – as the rational ego starves and wilts when it loses touch with intuition. When Marcel tastes the madeleine dipped in tea, he experiences in a flash of insight the absurdity of this situation.

This is the essence of the problem: 'losing touch'. But what is the solution? I grasp it instinctively whenever something interests me deeply. My rational ego is eager to pursue the matter, but it makes quite sure that the intuitions are not left behind. I can observe the same process when I am listening to music or enjoying poetry. I deliberately slow down the left-brain ego; I 'pay attention', I try to apprehend it simultaneously with reason and intuition, with the mind and the emotions. And if I can persuade them to cooperate, I suddenly find that I am grasping reality in a new way. It has taken on a third dimension – a dimension *of reality*. And this is enough to make me aware that what I normally take for reality is not real at all. It is a mere surface, a kind of stage scenery. It bears the same relation to reality that paste jewellery bears to real diamonds.

Now *this* is obviously the experience that Plato was speaking about – when the prisoner is unchained and taken out into the sunlight. Reason *can* prevent us from taking the shadows for reality. Proust spent most of his life in a state of emotional upheaval. The whole central episode of his novel – the love affair with Albertine – is an example of neurotic self-indulgence. Proust recognized that this tendency became dominant when his mother failed to kiss him goodnight, and he was allowed to spend the night in her bed. He possessed an exceptionally powerful intellect; but it was the slave of his emotions. Plato recognized that most men are the slaves of emotion and impulse and physical sensation; this is why he emphasized the importance of reason. But reason cannot produce the flash of 'absurd good news', the peak experience. It can only point us in the right direction.

The crucial step is to recognize the 'negative intentionality' that produces these confusions, and that leads inevitably to the process of 'losing touch'. Most practical activities involve some element of obsession. Let us say that I have decided to write a letter before dinner. As I write, I begin to feel hungry. Nevertheless, I tell myself that I shall enjoy my food more when I know the letter is finished; so I press on. Finally, I feel rather depressed and exhausted. And when I re-read the letter the next day, after a good night's sleep, I can see that I have allowed my hunger to influence my mood, and that this is reflected in the opinions I express.

What has happened is that my hunger has started a process of 'negative feedback'. It has made me feel that it is not worth making much effort; this in turn has reduced my pleasure in writing, which in turn increases my feeling of boredom and impatience. I *allow* myself to make less and less effort, yet I fail to see the connection between this act of 'rejection', of impatience, and my increasing boredom. I feel that the letter *is* boring. In other words, I feel that I am reacting in a rational and logical way to an obstacle in the external world. As my pressure sinks, I fail to see that *I* am releasing it, as deliberately as if I had pushed a matchstick into the valve of a tyre.

The real problem is that the process tends to be self-perpetuating. Modern man is permanently in a hurry. Because I am in a hurry, I fail to bring enough energy and concentration to bear on some specific task, and the task begins to strike me as futile and boring. And since most of my life is made up of similar tasks, I experience this mildly irritating sense of boredom from morning till night; I begin to accept it as the basic condition of modern life. My attitude becomes a habit. I contemplate tomorrow and tomorrow and tomorrow, and suddenly I wonder if it is all really worth the effort. Is this dreary repetition what they mean by 'living'? And as my 'heart sinks', I realize that if this state of boredom persists, then I am going to lose my grip on life. I may begin to experience a strangled sense of panic, of futility, a terrified conviction that life is 'vanity of vanities'. And because I lack insight into the process of negative intentionality, I remain totally unaware that all this is an absurd misunderstanding.

We also have tantalizing flashes of insight into how easy it would be to reverse the whole process. Something strikes me as so interesting that I focus upon it the total weight of my attention. Suddenly, I experience a curious inner glow, a refreshing trickle of optimism and excitement. Involuntarily, my attention increases. For a moment, I glimpse the astonishing truth that I merely have to *put* 'interest' into any experience in order to make it 'interesting'. For a moment, I grasp that the power and the glory lie behind my eyes. But this insight is altogether too strange, too bewildering, and a moment later, I have slipped back into the old habit of passivity.

But there are also times when this experience can be held on to. Perhaps, like Proust, I come to associate happiness with a particular place – or, like a child at Christmas, with some particular time. Because I am convinced that the place *is* interesting, I increase the intensity of my gaze; and this has the effect of bringing an instant, delicious flash of meaning, like the faint tingle that occurs when you place your tongue against the terminal of a torch battery. It may happen when I listen to a particular piece of music, or encounter a certain smell or taste. When my senses have become sharpened and focused in this manner, they may surprise me by producing unexpected flashes of intensity. I peer into the salad to see whether there is any avocado left, and suddenly the green of the lettuce and the red of the radishes and tomatoes glows and deepens, and the colours enter into combination with the smell of vinegar to produce that same deep, satisfying sense of reality that Proust experienced in the Champs Élysées, a feeling of delight that they merely exist. In such moments we become aware that our 'normal consciousness' consists mainly of a buzzing cloud of emotions like a swarm of gnats, and that most of them are completely unnecessary. It is then that we glimpse the truth that 'interest' has nothing to do with circumstances; that the view from a yacht in the Mediterranean or the edge of the Grand Canyon is no more interesting than the view of a gasworks in Manchester or the cracks in an old shoe. For the length of the insight, the phrase 'perception is intentional' becomes a more exciting piece of good news than anything in the world's scriptures.

And now we are near the very heart of the matter, the fundamental mechanisms of visionary consciousness. Let me try to clarify them with a case history.

In October 1975, an eighteen-year-old student named Robert Poulin walked into the classroom of his school in Ottawa, and opened fire with a shotgun, wounding seven students. Then he turned the gun on himself and blew his brains out. Poulin lived in the basement of his parents' home; his mother found smoke pouring from the window and alerted the fire brigade. They discovered the half-burnt corpse of a seventeen-year-old girl on the bed; she had been raped and stabbed to death. Poulin had apparently spoken to her at the bus stop – she was a neighbour – and persuaded her that he had something important to show her in his basement.

Police discovered piles of sex magazines, a box of women's underwear, hard core pornography, and a blow-up sex doll. Poulin's diary made it clear that he had been brooding about sex for a long time, and that he believed himself to be unattractive to women. He decided that, sooner or later, he would have to commit a rape. When he bought the sex doll for $30, he confided to his diary: 'Now I no longer think I will have to rape a girl. . . .' But on the day the doll arrived, he noted: 'Doll a big disappointment.'

We may also surmise that his final hours with seventeen-year-old Kim Rabot – a girl whose name was included in a list of possible rape victims – were also an anti-climax. He had been brooding and dreaming about sex for years; it was a subject that was permanently in his thoughts. Obviously, he expected 'the real thing' to be some kind of tremendous revelation, an almost mystical ecstasy. It would have been impossible for any experience to have lived up to such expectations. After the rape, he must have felt like the victim of a confidence trickster. There was a bloody naked corpse on the bed, somehow too real, too ordinary, to be sexually exciting. Then what had happened to the fever, the desire, the ecstasy? It must have seemed total illusion – part of life's strategy to ensure the continuation of the species. For a man who has 'seen through' the fraud, suicide must have seemed the only solution.

Poulin is abnormal, yet his story is only 'normal' experience magnified fifty times. We are all familiar with the way that reality seems an anti-climax after our expectations. A child looks forward to a birthday present for months, yet feels bored with it within days, even hours. We seem to spend a great deal of our lives saying, 'Is that all?' Disappointments are usually small and quickly forgotten, but they occur with great frequency. In fact, you could say that they are part of the essential texture of experience. Disappointment seems built into the sex act itself. A man who catches a glimpse of a girl taking off her clothes feels that she is infinitely desirable, yet if he makes love to her, he realizes that this is *not* the girl who caused him so much excitement. It is as if a swindler has cunningly substituted a paste jewel for a real one, or bundles of paper for pound notes. As Poulin tried to make love to his blow-up doll, it must have struck him that sex is largely our imagination. Yet he still believed that a real girl would deliver the promised ecstasy. If this failed to materialize, the result must have been conviction that life is a tissue of illusions. The feeling was given its definitive expression in literature in Villiers de l'Isle-Adam's *Axel*, where the hero persuades a girl to enter into a suicide pact on the grounds that no reality ever lives up to its promise, and that even their love will degenerate into a mere 'relationship'.

Yet before we accept this horribly plausible notion, we

should also recall those moments when an experience *did* live up to expectation. If life is an illusion, how can we account for these? And what of the experiences that came as a pleasant surprise, when we were not expecting them, and that seemed oddly perfect, without a note of discord? If we analyse such experiences, we can see that this was because there was no inner conflict, no 'mistrust', no element of doubt. In fact, the experiences that seem 'unreal' or disappointing are those in which we allow ourselves to remain, to some extent, passive spectators. Once we become involved, once we throw the weight of our own enthusiasm and vitality into the experience, it becomes self-evidently real and satisfying.

As soon as we begin to examine this problem through the microscope of phenomenology – the detached observation of inner states – we can begin to observe Moskvitin's 'visionary mechanisms' in action. Moskvitin recognized that it is *we* who transform the 'sparks', the raw material of perception, into what we actually see. Perception is a sculptor, a moulder of reality.

Let us examine this mechanism more closely. It is again important to grasp that the statement that '*we* transform the raw material' does *not* mean that we create reality. The meaning is already there. When I bite into an apple, I know that it will taste like an apple; even if I try to convince myself that it is an orange or a pear, it will still taste like an apple. The taste is already there. All I can do is to increase or decrease its taste, like turning the volume knob on a radio up or down. If I am anxious and preoccupied, I may not even notice whether it is an apple or a pear. But if I am hungry, and I concentrate my full attention on the apple, I can experience its smell, its texture, its flavour, so that it becomes the most delicious apple I have ever tasted.

Perception, then, is intentional; I fire it like an arrow. If I am feeling bored and passive, then I can scarcely muster the energy to pull back the string, and the arrow falls a few feet away. But if my expected reward – the taste of the apple or of a girl's lips – fills me with desire, I draw the bowstring back as far as it will go, and the arrow thuds into its target.

In many cases, I add this element of vitality so spontaneously that I am unaware that I am doing so. I go for a walk on a spring morning. The air smells so pleasant, the breeze is so fresh, that my senses reach out eagerly for experience. I am only half-aware of this intentional element, and am inclined to attribute my pleasure to some other cause – that it has been a long winter, that I have had a good night's sleep, that this morning really *is* exceptionally fresh. . . . The next day I take the same walk and find it disappointing. In fact, my conviction that I have only to relax and enjoy myself means that I am putting less vitality into the experience. Perhaps I read some depressing item in the morning paper before I came out, and this makes me feel: 'All this loveliness is an illusion – life is really rather grim . . .,' and the element of 'mistrust' makes me 'shrink' from the experience instead of running to meet it, as I did the previous day.

My own view of myself, my 'self-image', also plays an important part in my response to experience. Robert Poulin was a shy teenager, riddled with self-doubt. He spent a great deal of his time bored and exhausted, shrinking from direct experience, preferring the world of his imagination. So even if his victim had been willing to cooperate, he would have been in no position to get the most from the experience. The element of 'mistrust' would thrown him into an automatic stance of embarrassment and passivity. He would have failed to throw the weight of intentionality into the experience, like a boxer failing to put his weight into a punch. This is what Eliot was talking about in 'The Hollow Men':

> Between the idea
> And the reality . . .
> Between the emotion
> And the response
> Falls the shadow

The 'shadow' is the twinge of mistrust, the 'shrinking', the conviction that this is all an illusion. . . .

The male who is convinced that the female is his by right – or, for that matter vice versa – throws the full weight of his conviction into the experience and, as a result, finds it far more satisfying. (Even so, he may allow his intentionality to become diluted by force of habit, or by some other tension or preoccupation, and so lose the essence of the experience.)

We are speaking now of the basic 'intentional rule' that governs all experience. We can see it in operation when we lie in bed on a cold winter morning, knowing we have to get up in five minutes. We observe it when we sink into a hot bath after a hard day's work. We simply allow the mind to focus upon our present situation, instead of 'wandering'. We can see the principle in operation in the story of Tom Sawyer whitewashing the fence. Tom does not want to whitewash the fence; he wants to be elsewhere. So his mind is 'elsewhere', and he finds the task unrewarding. But by whistling and looking happy, he convinces his friends that he is enjoying himself. And when they have bribed him into letting them take turns, *they* actually enjoy it. Why? Because, expecting to enjoy it, they focus wholly upon the experience; their minds are not 'elsewhere'. It is as if they are holding up a mirror in which they can see their own faces.

A sense of optimism does it just as effectively. We have all observed how, after we have received some good news, the world seems to take on a warmer, richer colouring. If this experience is analysed more closely, it can be seen that the good news has filled us with a conviction that the world is a delightful place, *full of hidden meanings*. It is the attitude that children take towards experience: an assumption that whatever happens is bound to be interesting.

And if I take the trouble to observe myself in these moods of expectancy and receptivity, I notice something else. I am now free of 'doubt', of the 'shadow', of the *assumption of meaninglessness* that so often drains me of optimism and vitality. When I become aware of this, I can see that this assumption is not a conscious belief – as it must have been when Poulin decided on suicide. It is a tacit assumption, a kind of hesitancy. But it has upon my consciousness exactly the same effect that self-doubt would have upon an actor delivering his lines or a pianist interpreting a Beethoven sonata: it somehow robs the whole thing of conviction. This is what Blake meant when he wrote:

> If the sun and moon should doubt
> They'd immediately go out.

He recognized that 'doubt' is not simply a matter of the intellect, but is woven into the fabric of consciousness. Goethe was expressing the same insight when he made Mephistopheles describe himself as 'the spirit that negates'.

But what is the precise nature of this 'doubt'? Kierkegaard would say that it is the essential *'angst'* of the human spirit contemplating the mystery of its existence; Sartre would say that it is a recognition that consciousness is a kind of emptiness; Samuel Beckett would say it is man's realization that life has no meaning. But in that case, how do we explain moments like Proust's 'glimpse' in the Champs-Élysées, which make the doubts seem suddenly absurd?

This question forms the subject of a remarkable essay called 'The Process of Thought', which was presented to the American Society for Clinical Hypnosis in 1971 by Dr Howard B. Miller. I have written of Miller elsewhere,* so shall here offer only a brief summary of his central idea. When studying the curative powers of hypnosis, Miller was led to ask what factor in the nervous system explains why a person under deep hypnosis can control bleeding and even certain diseases. This led him into considering the philosophical question: what is thought? The psychologist's answer to that question is: the flow of images, ideas, emotions, that take place when the brain is conscious. Miller concluded that this definition is inadequate; he wrote: 'However, research and experiments have led me to consider and propose the existence of a powerful factor *behind* this so-called stream of thought. This power seems to be a controlling and creative one. . . .' When we close our eyes and look inside ourselves, says Miller, we seem to be watching a kind of television screen, on which appears a continually changing flux of symbols, emotions and pictures. But *who is looking at the screen?* Who is this 'you' who is observing it?

He goes on to mention Wilder Penfield's experiments in which an electronic probe, touching certain areas of the brain during surgery, can cause the patient to re-live, in the utmost detail, events from the past. The brain is obviously a gigantic library, a computer with an incredible amount of storage space.

* *Frankenstein's Castle*, p. 104 et seq. See also my introduction to *A Directory of Possibilities*.

And this, says Miller, is our problem. As Proust knew only too well, the computer cannot be persuaded to allow us immediate access to 'remembrance of things past'. Moreover, it seems to prefer to fill our heads with thoughts and images we could well do without. And when I would prefer to taking mental voyages, it keeps me drearily trapped in the present. I am supposed to be the master of my brain and body; in fact, I seem to be their slave. No wonder philosophers are always asking 'Who am I?' It is the cry of despair of a man who is not master in his own house. . . .

This, says Miller, is a mistake of enormous magnitude, the mistake that lies at the heart of all our problems. To begin to recognize this mistake, we only have to close our eyes and proceed to conjure up different scenes – yourself on the beach, complete with the smell of seaweed and the warmth of the sun, then yourself at the foot of a mountain, standing in the snow and looking up at the clouds. . . . We ourselves select and change the image on the television screen. The observer who looks at the screen is 'the essential you' – or, as Miller prefers to call it, 'the Unit of Pure Thought'. Our mental processes seem confused and random – like a cinema projector running wild – only because we fail to make the effort of control. Thoughts are controlled and created by the Unit of Pure Thought, the 'You'. It is the lack of this awareness, says Miller, that has prevented us from picking up the reins and taking control of our own brains.

Miller's ideas are very closely connected indeed with that central recognition of Husserl that thought is intentional, and with Moskvitin's insight into the way in which a kind of hidden artist 'paints' reality in front of our eyes. But Miller has gone boldly to the heart of the matter, and stated: '*You* are the master of your brain and your thoughts.'

How did we get into this confused situation? For millions of years, human evolution trained us for *action*, not for thought. When a hunter is engaged in the excitement of the chase, he does not need to ask, 'Who am I?' He knows. He is aware of *his* power to transform reality, that he decides whether the spear will plunge into the animal's side or its neck. His 'I' *knows* it is in control. Modern man feels the same when he is driving at ninety miles an hour or peering down the sights of a rifle. But when he is standing on a train, clinging to a strap, or waiting for the traffic lights to change, he becomes passive. He spends so much of his life regarding himself as passive – 'mediocre, accidental mortal' – that it becomes a part of his self-image, something he is inclined to accept as a basic premise of his existence. So when certain situations make him aware that he *is* the 'master' – love-making, drinking, fast driving – he is inclined to regard these insights as some kind of pleasant delusion. And he attempts to duplicate them by simply repeating the experience, and sometimes becoming an alcoholic or a traffic fatality in the process.

It is true that thinking *can* produce the same sense of mastery, but this is such a recent activity in the evolutionary time-scale that most of us do it hesitantly and badly. Thinking seldom involves much sense of urgency, so we fail to do it with much conviction. The result is that it has become a primarily left-brain activity – whereas in fact, real thinking, the kind we encounter in the dialogues of Plato, involves the close cooperation of both halves of the brain – like two men at either end of a double-handed saw.

Miller believes that we have the power to change the situation. We can use thought to explore and analyse all our other vital processes. And once we have achieved the insight that thought is 'intentional', we can begin to use it to control our perceptions and feelings. The history of religion teaches us that such an insight really can enable us to gain control. If Proust had really grasped the meaning of his own insight – that he was *not* accidental, mediocre, mortal – he would have been able to duplicate the experience at will, instead of waiting for it to occur by chance. The Hindu mystic Ramakrishna *was* able to grasp the meaning of the insight when, in a state of despair, he tried to kill himself with a sword, and experienced the vision of meaning that Graham Greene experienced when he played Russian roulette; but Greene, like Proust, failed to hold on to the meaning, while Ramakrishna was able to summon it at will, producing states of visionary ecstasy. These violent methods, while obviously effective, are dangerous. The essence of the Buddha's teaching is that we can achieve insight – 'enlightenment' – simply by learning to use the mind and will correctly. Violent methods – even the self-torment of the Christian ascetics – is quite unnecessary. And what is so exciting about the insights of

Hudson, Maslow, Sperry, Ornstein, Miller is that they reveal the existence of a scientific route to 'enlightenment'. Perhaps the most unexpected development of our time is that religion and science are ceasing to point in opposite directions.

The essence of these insights always amounts to the same thing: that our mental and physical states are far more within our control than we realize. The human situation could be compared to that of a passenger in a car that gets stuck in the mud, and who is asked by the driver to give it a push. But he is convinced that he is too weak to be of any use; so he pushes half-heartedly, and his conviction is reinforced when nothing happens. But finally, driven to efforts by shouts of 'Push!', he exerts all his strength, and the car shoots forward. And from then on, he will never make the mistake of assuming he is impotent.

An example of this process is cited by Abraham Maslow. When he began talking to his students about 'peak experiences', they began to recollect peak experiences from their own lives – experiences that they had already half forgotten. And as soon as they made a habit of thinking and talking about peak experiences, they began having peak experiences all the time. The peak experience is, in fact, merely 'committed' experience, experience in which the ego exerts its full weight, instead of 'hanging back' in the conviction that it is merely a spectator. As soon as Maslow's students began to recall past peak experiences, they discovered that 'peaks' are not some kind of divine visitation. *We* cause them by being optimistic and interested.

We also cause the opposite of the peak experience: the sinking feeling, the sudden sense of mistrust. This is based upon the conviction that life is an endless struggle against impossible odds, a drearily repetitious obstacle race. This is dangerous because it looks so plausible; for indeed, life *does* consist mainly of repetition. And in moods of optimism, we see that this is no reason for despondency. A great actor can transform *Hamlet* into a new play; a great conductor can make the Beethoven Fifth sound as if it is being played for the first time. It is no objection to these works to say that they consist of a repetition of the same words or notes. On the contrary: the fact that they already exist on paper allows the interpreter a degree of freedom that would be impossible if he were forced to improvise.

We *must* grasp this central fact: that most of our problems are self-inflicted, caused by 'negative feedback'. We allow some dreary prospect to cause a sinking feeling, then accept the sinking feeling as evidence that life is difficult and dangerous – 'We can't win.' Our descendants will look back with astonishment on our naivety. They will have learned the crucial lesson: that external events may or may not be controllable; *we* choose our reaction to them.

7

Access to Inner Worlds

And what of the subject stated in the title of this book: access to inner worlds?

Consider what happens if I attempt to recall a tune. I place myself in a receptive frame of mind, and address a kind of question to my memory. And if I am relaxed and receptive, memory will send up the answer immediately. The tune is already 'inside' me. Proust's taste of the cake dipped in herb tea was a revelation of the size of this inner library. And Proust, for all his irritating qualities, deserves credit for being the first great novelist to make this experience the centre of his life's work. He raises the most interesting of all questions: what is the meaning of that overwhelming certainty that 'all is well'? For Proust, the paradox was that it was a feeling of strength and confidence; and, since Proust was a hypochondriac, this contradicted the image of himself that he took completely for granted. Nietzsche experienced a similar revelation during a thunderstorm on a hilltop; as the thunder crashed and the rain hammered on the roof of the hut in which he had taken shelter, he felt an immense exhilaration, and wrote: 'Pure will, without the troubles and perplexities of intellect – how happy, how free!' Yet Nietzsche, like Proust, suffered from poor health, and the revelation seemed to be a contradiction of a self-evident 'truth' about himself. The revelation always has this effect of paradox, of flat contradiction of our normal values. Gorki tells how Tolstoy was walking down the street when two guardsmen came walking towards him. As they strode along with jingling spurs

115

Tolstoy said indignantly: 'What pompous stupidity, like circus animals. . . .' Then, as the soldiers came abreast, marching in step, 'But aren't they magnificent!' Sheer vital energy overwhelmed his intellectual judgement; the right brain contradicted the left.

All of which makes it clear that the certainty that 'all is well' is a recognition of this 'other self', with its immense, crude vitality. Man has slowly developed a left-brain personality, capable of dealing with the intricate minutiae of existence – unlike animals and young children, who are quite incapable of handling complications. As the complexity of civilization has increased, and survival of the fittest has ensured the development of left-brain efficiency, the left brain has come to seem the 'dominant hemisphere' and the right correspondingly the 'minor hemisphere'. The right has slipped into the position of an overworked housewife, a downtrodden drudge.

For most of the time, this hardly matters, for the right carries on with its essential task of supplying 'reality' with a third dimension, a dimension of meaning. When we are thoroughly relaxed – perhaps on holiday – the right is treated as an equal partner, and we are suddenly surprised to notice that reality can be so pleasant and rich. But the moment we are placed under stress, the left dispenses with this dimension of meaning, and contents itself with a symbolic representation of the world; these moving creatures who jostle me are merely 'people'; those noisy objects that roar past me are merely 'traffic'. In effect, the left is holding its breath, like a swimmer under water, making do without meaning. But if it does this for too long, it begins to feel tired and depressed. And at this point, as we have seen, this deadly 'negative feedback' mechanism slips into gear, and the result can be depression, panic attacks, nervous collapse, even insanity. ('Meaning starvation' – for example, sensory deprivation in a black room – can produce hallucinations, as the right brain tries to replace the missing dimension.)

Human beings have developed various ways of attempting to escape this negative feedback circuit. The simplest is to allow our instincts to take over: eating, drinking, hunting, making love, making war, seeking adventure. All these activities can rescue us from left-brain impoverishment. But the left brain has its own remedies, ways of *reminding* itself that the impoverished, two-dimensional reality is not the whole truth. The most powerful and effective of these methods is religion, which requires the recognition, as an article of faith, that there *is* another dimension of reality beyond this world which is visible to our senses. So when the savage has completed his ritual sacrifice to his gods, or when a man rises from his knees after the Sacrament, he experiences a sense of comfort, of release from anxiety, of contact with meaning and purpose.

Later still, man developed art as a method of 'reminding' himself of that other dimension. It originated as a servant of religion, but eventually assumed its own identity. Art is, in fact, a collaboration between the right and left hemispheres; the right provides the insights, the left translates them into words or shapes or musical notes. Keats pointed out that the essence of art – he was speaking of poetry but it applies to all art – is 'negative capability', openness, receptivity, when the left brain is prepared to remain silent and wait for the right to speak. Since art is a collaboration between left and right, it can hardly avoid serving as a reminder of the existence of the right.

Science came later than religion or art, and in the past century, has gained itself a bad reputation among the religious and the artistically inclined. But this is because scientists have taken it upon themselves to dogmatize about reality, unaware that the reality they perceive through their microscopes is the two-dimensional reality of the left brain. Science is nothing more than a reference system, like the index at the end of a book, which is meaningless without the reality that occupies the rest of the book. And now this slow, plodding method of 'indexing' reality is beginning to reveal its true value. For the left brain is never entirely convinced by the 'revelations' of religion and art; it is inclined to discount them as mere 'emotions'. But today its own investigations of the structure of the brain have made it aware that reality is unreal until it is completed by a third dimension.

And so we have been enabled to grasp through the intellect the truth we already knew by instinct: that if the left brain is to grasp the reality of the world, it must slow down until it is walking at the same pace as the right. For the first time, we are able to grasp objectively what happened when the romantics experienced their 'moments of vision', and why they found them so dishearteningly elusive. We can also see the baffling nature of the problem faced by the romantics. They were, in effect, trying to re-live the whole history of mankind. Animals are instinctive, right-brain creatures, who have no capacity for self-detachment. But at least they remain in constant contact with the three-dimensional world of reality. When human beings leave their childhood behind, they have to learn to cope with a world of symbols; and so they lose hold of their sense of reality. The romantics discovered how to use art to restore the contact; but in doing so, they were inclined to drift back into the world of the child. Thomas Mann describes in *Buddenbrooks* how young Hanno Buddenbrook loves his holidays at the seaside; yet his family can never understand why these holidays seem to leave him weaker, not stronger. It is because a return to right-brain reality creates a revulsion from the left. The romantics thought that this was inevitable: that the man who is capable of experiencing this deeper reality (and it *is* deeper in the quite literal sense of possessing a third dimension) will inevitably be a 'loser'. It became part of the romantic myth that man can choose either crude vitality and success, or sensitivity and failure. From Blake to D.H. Lawrence, the romantics were united in denouncing the left brain and all its works.

We can see that the conflict was quite unnecessary. It is not a choice between going forward into the world of the scientist or backward into the world of the child. Left-brain consciousness must remain as dominant and powerful as ever, prepared to take over at a moment's notice. Yet it must also be capable of remaining silent; of suspending its dominance to allow the right to develop its own powers of self-expression.

Now we can see the implications of Brad's experiences. One of the main problems of western man is that his left brain is hyperactive. Like some enormous factory, it hums and roars with deafening activity. Yet much of this activity is automatic; machines have been left running when they could equally well be switched off.

When we are subjected to unexpected stress or sudden crisis, the factory noise rises to a hysterical crescendo. Disappearance of the stress brings a startling silence, as we become aware that the anxiety is unnecessary – and that the normal level of tension is far in excess of our need for alertness. We realize we could *afford* to relax and treat life as a holiday. This mechanism explains Greene's 'vision' after playing Russian roulette.

There is another method of silencing the machinery – to remain relaxed but alert for fairly long periods of time – which is the basis of the technique of enlightenment discovered by the Buddha. He dismissed the strenuous self-torment of Hindu ascetics and yogis, and insisted that it was enough to sit quietly, holding the mind calm and steady. 'This trembling, wavering mind, so difficult to guard and to control, this the wise man makes straight as the fletcher straightens his shaft.' 'Will is the way to Nirvana; laziness is the way of death. The wise man guards his vigour as his greatest possession.' But one of the chief difficulties encountered by those who try to meditate – to silence the mind – is our tendency to drift into 'free association'. As Brad lay beside his wife, there was no tendency to free association; he was listening intently for the first signs that she was returning to normal. He was, in effect, asking his mind to be quiet. He was like a man listening intently for a distant sound. After a while, his mind obeyed; and then 'listening' became a habit. And at that point, Brad had achieved his own version of enlightenment. From now on, the other self could make itself heard.

Brad's method, like the Buddha's, is fundamentally simple and easy to use. As soon as we relax and close our eyes, we become conscious of the roar of the machinery, the tension of the body, the forward-drive of the will. It is the opposite of what you experience when you awaken from a deep sleep, thoroughly relaxed. But the aim is *not* now to relax. It is to bring the automatic activity of the mind under control, to silence the machinery.

Since we are full of automatic tensions, the direct approach – simply to 'unwind' – is seldom successful. It is better to begin by deliberately increasing the tension. Concentrate the mind, as if lifting an enormously heavy weight, and allow the attention to move from part to part of the body, enlisting the cooperation of each part in the collective effort. Clench and unclench the fists; tense and relax the muscles of the arms, the stomach, the thighs. After half a minute or so, relax. Then do it again.

My own experience is that after ten minutes or so there is a sense of a tidal flow of energy around the body. Mesmer believed that the universe is full of vital currents, and that human beings can tune in to these currents. Certainly, the sensation produced by this constant effort of 'vigilance' is of waves of energy running through the body like an in-coming tide.

This effort also makes one aware that we are normally full of unused energy. If I am forced to keep breaking off my writing to check facts in reference books, I become aware of an increasing exasperation; it is rather like holding my breath. These 'trapped' energies can produce migraine or depression. The exercise of 'controlled tension' makes one aware of these energies, as they are slowly discharged. A point comes at which so much 'trapped' energy has been discharged that we can afford to relax. And now, like a tired athlete, we can accept relaxation with gratitude, and without the protesting voice of unused energies.

This is an interesting state. For once the protesting voices have been silenced, there is nothing to prevent us from opening the door and walking into the world inside us.

This can be a stage of delightful exploration. In a story called 'The Man of the Crowd', Edgar Allan Poe describes how, recovering from an illness, he sat in the window of a coffee house in London. 'With returning strength, I found myself in one of those happy moods which are so precisely the converse of *ennui* – moods of the keenest appetency, when the film from the mental vision departs. . . .' In this case, illness had switched off the 'machinery', and returning health had not yet switched it on. Poe describes his immense interest as he studied the passing crowds. But in the same state, we can study the passing crowds inside the mind. It is my own experience that in these states, mental pictures are exceptionally clear. The sensation is not unlike getting a good picture on a television screen on which we have become accustomed to poor reception. And suddenly, it becomes obvious that this world has been there all the time, waiting for us to enter. It is like some cave in the Arabian Nights, entered by raising a massive stone slab. And below the slab there is a flight of stone steps, leading down to an underground palace.

It is important to grasp that we are not now speaking of a world of dreams or fancies. Sir Karl Popper made this point when he coined the term 'World 3'. World 1 is the physical world outside us; World 2 is the subjective world of which we become aware when we close our eyes. But then, there is the world that man has created or discovered, and which he stores in libraries. If our civilization was destroyed tomorrow, but all the books were still left intact, it would be possible for our descendants to rebuild the world within a few generations. But if all the books and records were also destroyed, man would have to start from scratch, and it might take two thousand years or so. World 3, the world of what we have discovered, is an independent entity, like World 1 and 2. It has objective existence, like the physical world.

Those who have succeeded in gaining 'access to inner worlds' have discovered with surprise that they are quite unlike dreams or hallucinations. In *Heaven and Hell*, Aldous Huxley made this point in a now-famous remark: 'Like the earth of a hundred years ago, our mind still has its darkest Africas, its unmapped Borneos and Amazonian basins.' And he adds: 'Like the giraffe and the duck-billed platypus, the creatures inhabiting these remoter regions of the mind are exceedingly improbable. Nevertheless they exist. . . .' He goes on to point out that some people can be transported to these regions under hypnosis. Huxley comments that we are still ignorant of how hypnosis produces its effects. Since he wrote these words, in 1956, we have a fairly shrewd idea of how it produces its effects: by putting the left brain to sleep, and leaving the right wide awake. And, as we know, either putting the left brain to sleep, or silencing the noise of its machinery, can open the doors to the world inside us.

Huxley's simile about our mental Borneos and Amazonian basins may be too picturesque. The first thing we discover when the left brain can be persuaded to let go of our coat tails is that we are in a large and rather interesting library. Yet it differs from an ordinary library in one basic respect. In libraries, the books sit on the shelves, with their backs to you, and you have no way of finding out about their contents except by removing them and looking inside. But this mental library is rather more like a sound library where the records are being played continuously. If you place your ear close to the covers of any book, you can hear the memories it contains. Perhaps you catch the sound of a music box that belonged to your elder sister when you were a baby, or the long-forgotten barking of the hysterical pekinese they used to have next door, or the warm, tarry smell of the garden fence in the sunlight, together with a vivid memory of the way the paint blistered on the back door, or the reflections of light on the boating pond in the park, or the taste of over-roasted chestnuts that burnt the tongue. . . . Even the briefest glimpse of these memories produces a sense of pure delight and astonishment, that feeling of 'immortality' that Proust described. And why do we feel astonished? To begin with, because the sheer profusion, the sheer quantity, of these memories seems unnecessary. *Why* has the brain carefully stored up everything that has ever happened to us since birth, if we are never going to make use of it, and if the brain is going to start decomposing within minutes of death? Somehow, this seems unlikely. There *must* be some other purpose behind human existence, some immense, complex, unfathomable purpose. . . . This is not a reasoned conclusion; it is a feeling, a kind of perception, and it explains why Proust ceased to feel mediocre, accidental, mortal, and why Camus's Meursault could suddenly realize that he had been happy and was happy still. It explains why Scrooge burst into tears and ceased to be a miser when he had been allowed a brief glimpse of that library inside the head.

But this library inside us is not merely a repository of separate memories. What is so exciting is that these memories can blend together and connect into something much bigger. The tarry smell of the sun-warmed fence is connected with the smell of grass, and an odd cold sensation that seems to be a memory of water, which in turn brings back the cold of a winter day and the sogginess of melting snow. . . . And at this point, it becomes difficult to pinpoint the sensations because they seem to be spreading outwards, so that every one evokes half a dozen others, and so on in geometric progression. There is a dazzling sensation of hovering above your own life, seeing it as a whole, like some enormous landscape. And as we glimpse these 'distant horizons', we also become aware that *this* is what memory is *for*. Not fragmentary, piecemeal perceptions, but a total grasp. And not only of my own life, but, by some process of deduction, of other lives, of all life.

Our 'normal' way of perceiving the world could be compared to a man who is so short-sighted that, whenever he goes to a picture gallery, he has to peer at the paintings through a magnifying glass. Naturally, he can never see more than a few square inches. If he is very intelligent and very diligent, he *can* put together a general idea of the whole picture. But if he tries to stand back and see it as a whole, it turns into a blur. If someone presented him with a pair of powerful spectacles that would enable him to look at pictures from the proper distance, the result would be a revelation – very much like Plato's image of the man who is allowed outside the cave.

The absurd thing is that, in the case of this inner picture gallery, we know there is nothing wrong with our eyesight. We were intended to have these glimpses of things as a whole. Then what is it that prevents us? The answer seems to be our lack of desire, our failing to recognize that this *is* one of our perfectly normal possibilities. We take it for granted that living means 'coping' with the external world, and that the moments of relaxation, when we retreat inside ourselves, are no more than 'breathing spaces', holidays from the everyday business of living. All children know better, of course. When they become absorbed in a fairy tale, with its magical landscapes, they know perfectly well that life was intended to be more than this dreary business of 'living'. They know precisely what William Blake meant when he wrote:

> Father, O father, what do we here
> In this land of unbelief and fear?
> The Land of Dreams is better far,
> Above the light of the morning star.

They feel increasingly that this world is a kind of prison. Yet there genuinely seems to be no alternative. Their fathers have to go out to work to support them, and they, in due course, will have to learn to force this difficult world to grant them subsistence. So they also learn to 'cope', and to take brief holidays in the 'land of dreams'.

This certainly seems to be inevitable. Man has become the most dominant creature on earth because he has learned to 'cope' better than any other animal. And animals certainly have very little capacity for 'access to inner worlds'. When a stranger comes into your house, your dog either recognizes him or he doesn't. The dog has no capacity to search his memory or ask, 'Now where have I seen him before?' It seems reasonable to suppose that man's memory, that rudimentary access to inner worlds, is simply one more evolutionary development to enable him to 'cope'.

Those deeper glimpses of 'inner worlds' reveal that this is not so. If we possess such a vast inner library, were we not intended to make more use of it than we do? We were intended to have a deeper, more vivid type of consciousness. But how are we to achieve it? Brad's experience leaves no possible doubt about the answer. We have to *know* the library is there, and start using it. We have to learn deep relaxation, learn to still the left brain and the senses. The Aladdin's cave is there, waiting for us to walk in. The only thing that stops us from doing so is ignorance of its existence.

And yet we cannot claim to be really ignorant. When, for example, I read Raskolnikov's statement that he would rather stand on a narrow ledge for ever and ever than die at once, I know perfectly well what he means, and I know I would feel the same. When I hear about some tramp who says that all he wants out of life is a country cottage with roses round the door and a small income, I understand exactly why he believes that this would keep him happy for the rest of his days. *In fact*, Raskolnikov would probably commit suicide after a few weeks on a narrow ledge; the tramp would probably become bored and dissatisfied after a winter in his ideal cottage. But a simple act of identification makes us aware of why they thought otherwise. The life of a hunted criminal is one of continual uncertainty; so is the life of a homeless tramp. They make continuous demands on the ability to 'cope'. And it is so easy to see how, when we have the chance to relax and appreciate life, we merely have to sigh with relief and *slow down*. If you asked Raskolnikov what he would do on his ledge, he would reply: 'Be grateful that I am still alive.' If you asked the tramp what he would do in his garden, he would reply: 'Just look around.' For each of them, the answer lies in simply calming the senses, slowing down the left brain until it walks at the same pace as the right.

This is only the first step. There is obviously far more to it than that. Consider more closely what happens when we 'slow down'. Let us suppose that I feel tired after a hard day's work. I pour myself a glass of wine, drop into my armchair, and heave a sigh of relief. In effect, I tell myself: now you can relax. It is a kind of hypnotic command. Then I pick up a novel. I read only one paragraph – a description of an autumn day – yet as I read, I seem to smell that distinctive smell of damp earth and rotting leaves. What has happened is that, because my left brain has slowed down, my right can perform its proper function of supplying a third dimension to experience. The experience is, in this case, purely fictional; yet the right hemisphere dutifully supplies those smells and sounds and colours. It can do so because I am in no hurry. I am prepared to listen without impatience.

If I push the book aside and stare out of the window, the right brain is just as willing to do its own specialized job. I get a feeling of dozens of possible sensations hovering on the edge of consciousness, like willing servants, ready to obey my instructions. If I choose to think about last year's holidays, I can close my eyes, and momentarily travel back to that rented cottage with its noisy plumbing and that dangerous back doorstep. But my right brain is just as willing to give me a glimpse of my schooldays, or the science lab at the technical college, complete with that acrid smell of nitrogen peroxide. If I choose to open a volume of poems, it will supply a 'third dimension' for a poem of Robert Service just as willingly as for W. H. Auden; the right brain is no cultural snob. And if I want to put on a record of a Haydn symphony, it will happily supply a whole kaleidoscope of images and impressions.

All these sensations clearly belong to the faculty called imagination. But we normally think of imagination as the ability to conjure up mental *images*: I can imagine what it would be like to win the football pools, or to go hang-gliding. In fact, imagination is far more than this. It is the ability to re-create experience, in all its complexity and richness. And the right brain is able to do precisely that.

The problem is that it seldom gets a chance. I read a book about ancient Rome, and imagine that I now have an excellent grasp of the world of the Romans. My right brain shakes its head in despair; if only I had allowed it to cooperate, it could have re-created ancient Rome for me. How? By drawing upon its immense store of memories and impressions. I have galloped through the book at such a speed that it is little more than a series of blurred impressions. But it is not simply a question of speed – the right can move with surprising speed when it wants to. It is a kind of forgetfulness. We forget that when we relax, the right brain will supply reality with a third dimension.

And now it becomes possible to understand the direction of human evolution. The 'reality' experienced by animals is no doubt far richer and more complex than our human reality, because they experience it with the whole brain, not just with a half. And their experiences are also stored away in the brain-library. But their access to this library is then limited. They lack reflective self-consciousness. It is doubtful whether a dog can lie on the mat and recall images of its past. It lacks any kind of detachment from itself.

The first step in human evolution was to achieve 'detachment'. Slowly, and no doubt very painfully, man learned to use his powers of reason. It must have been an uphill task, as hard as a child learning to cope with the adult world. But it was necessary to survival. Our ancestors had to learn how to ambush the mammoth and the great elk, and how to outwit the natural cunning of predators who wanted to make a meal of their children. Their success led to the creation of surprisingly complex societies, with shamans who taught them how to achieve success in the hunt by means of magic. The shamans eventually became priests, and cities sprang up around temples. Man had to learn to cope with a complex and 'unnatural' social life. Cities were intended to protect their inhabitants; but the archaeology of Mesopotamia teaches us that almost as soon as the first cities appeared – around 6000 BC – the first wars began. The city dwellers were squabbling about territory. No matter how hard he tried, it seemed that man could not escape stress and uncertainty. So he used his ingenuity to create cities with massive walls and underground water supplies, to withstand siege. He also created war chariots and siege engines to destroy other people's cities.

The result was that by the year 3000 BC, the history of mankind had turned into an almost continuous tale of slaughter. Three thousand years before the Nazis, the Assyrians practised torture and genocide, and boasted about them in their inscriptions and bas-reliefs. The fictional brutality of the James Bond novel shocks us; but if we imagine something of the sort happening continuously for century after century, we can begin to understand why man grew like a hot-house plant. To the student of early history, it seems incredible that Plato was writing the *Republic* only five thousand years after the foundation of the first cities. And that ten thousand years before that, our ancestors lived in caves. But it was almost certainly because human life was so bloody and violent that man developed the powers of his left brain, the ability to think, to calculate, to look ahead.

And now he possessed these powers, a new phase began. Spartans and Persians and Macedonians continued to slaughter one another and burn cities. But now so-called 'learned men' were studying the heavens and the forces of nature, and committing their observations to scrolls and sheepskins. Man began to build a new world, the world of knowledge – Popper's 'World 3'. And some remarkable men made a very creditable attempt to transfer the whole sum of human knowledge into their own small brains – their left brains. Nowadays, names like Paracelsus and Ficino and Pico della Mirandola and Cardano mean very little to us; in their own time, they were regarded as intellectual supermen. By the nineteenth century, such men were no longer a rarity; universities produced them by the dozen. Men like Kant, Hegel, Carlyle, Ruskin, Soloviev, Tolstoy, lived in World 3 as naturally as a fish lives in water, and so did thousands of 'intellectuals' we have never even heard of.

Yet such men were not necessarily happy in their self-chosen element; Ruskin even went insane. They despised mere physical existence; they wanted life raised to a higher level by the power of the mind. Yet most of them were thoroughly dissatisfied with their cold world of intellect. The romantics expressed this dissatisfaction most clearly: the longing for something warmer, richer, *more real*, than this attenuated realm of philosophy and art.

And we, at last, are in a position to understand precisely what they wanted. With their heads stuffed with all kinds of knowledge, they wanted to *make it live*, as Combray suddenly 'lived' for

Proust as he tasted the madeleine. That is why human beings have
such a passion for knowledge: because it somehow frees them from
the personal, allows them to enter a wider world where there is a
sense of freedom, like standing on a mountain top. This in turn
makes us aware of the extraordinary and paradoxical fact that
human beings were not primarily intended to live in 'this world'.
This sounds absurd; for when we look at a dog or a bird, we can see
plainly that its 'purpose' is to keep itself alive – to survive – and to
propagate its kind. That is its primary purpose and, as far as we can
see, its only obvious purpose. Man is an animal: ergo, the same
thing should apply to him. Yet human beings who are restricted to
such an existence feel there is something wrong. They begin to
crave some 'other' form of existence; this is the origin of religion.
And when we read of a Newton discovering the law of gravity, a
Harvey discovering the circulation of the blood, a Kant discovering that the mind influences our perceptions, a Freud discovering that man's unconscious mind is far more powerful than
his conscious mind, we see in a flash that man *was* intended for more
than mere survival. He was not intended for 'personal' existence;
he was intended for *impersonal* existence. This sounds bleak and
uncomfortable, but that is only because we are confusing the
impersonal with our left-brain, two-dimensional consciousness.
When the right brain adds its third dimension, the realm of the
impersonal becomes far *more* rich and exciting than the personal.
Ants labour impersonally at their ant-hills; wasps labour impersonally at their nests: these are their homes. Man labours impersonally at this gigantic edifice that is World 3: that is *his* home.

And now we come to the most absurd, the most preposterous
part of the story. What would we think of a man who lived out on
the lawn in a tent, while he built himself a magnificent home, and
then absent-mindedly went on living in the tent and left the house
empty? For that is precisely what man has done. We have only to
glance at the enormous volumes of history, philosophy, theology,
anthropology, sociology, on library shelves, to see that very few of
the writers actually *lived* their knowledge. Arnold Toynbee
admits as much in the last volume of *A Study of History*, where he
describes certain brief moments in which he experienced history as

a living reality. Those few moments of 'living history' were enough to provide the stimulus for half a century's labour. Similarly, Proust's few 'glimpses' led to the writing of his immense novel, and the writing itself was an attempt to fathom the mystery of those glimpses, with their tantalizing implication that it could all be 'so easy'. Proust created a masterpiece, yet he failed to solve the mystery.

But *why* does man live in a tent? Why does he treat the mansion as a museum which is open for only a few minutes a week? The answer probably lies in the past few thousand years, with its high level of violence. Man developed his intelligence to avoid extinction, and in the past few millennia, that threat has actually increased – its source being his own kind. So intelligence has developed in association with the need for alertness, for scanning the external world for problems and threats. In short, intelligence sprang from a sense of urgency. And now the urgency has diminished, and man can afford to relax and enjoy this magnificent civilization he has created, he finds it impossible to escape the old sense of urgency. Like a man who has been driving all day, and who keeps waking up at night, imagining he is still behind the wheel, mankind has slipped into an insidious habit – of anxiety, of tension, of over-alertness.

But intelligence *is* the ability to adjust to new circumstances. And compared to some of the problems he has solved in the past – problems of survival that make our own lives seem like a non-stop holiday – this problem of left-brain over-alertness is relatively trivial. It has remained so persistent largely because we have made no real attempt to solve it. When things are going well, we tend to switch on the 'automatic pilot', and do what we did yesterday and the day before. This is another legacy of the past: that we need crisis to keep alert. But when we consider this matter more closely, we realize that we already know the answer.

Let us first of all restate the problem. It is our inability to 'retreat inside ourselves', to make use of our freedom. We can be free and yet bored. And when we are bored, we feel trapped in this material world, 'as if that were all there is'. When we are faced with difficult problems, we know that to be without problems would in itself be delightful. But after being without problems for a day or two, we feel 'at a loose end'. It is infuriating to feel that you are a victim of your own moods, and that you lack the ability to carry out long-term decisions. This is why ascetics flagellated themselves and slept in hair shirts; they felt instinctively that the answer lay in self-discipline. Yet *we* feel instinctively that this is not the answer either; this is trying to open the door with a battering ram when it ought to open of its own accord.

The problem is 'generalized hypertension'; our minds refuse to stop running. Yet we possess a natural 'brake'. If someone raises his finger and says: 'Listen!', we automatically apply this brake and slow down our senses (another way of saying: sharpen our perceptions).

Again, consider what happens when you finally get hold of a book you have been wanting to read for a long time. You make sure that you will not be disturbed, and then 'switch off' your interest in the external world – so that if someone speaks to you, you don't even hear them. It is exactly as if you had taken a large funnel, inserted it into the book, and then poured all your attention into it.

Sex can have this same 'funnelling effect', concentrating the senses and focusing the vital energies, giving us again a glimpse of that Proustian sense of power and control. This is why sex means so much more to human beings than to any other animal. Equally revealing, from our point of view, is the popularity of pornography. After all, we enjoy eating, but few of us bother to read books about it. But the actuality of sex is often a disappointment. Why? Because it easily becomes diluted by habit – the robot. Our senses drift back into their old habit of 'scanning the external world'. And the quantity of attention that goes down the funnel diminishes steadily. A book enables us to by-pass the robot; we deliberately focus full attention on the description of sex, and again achieve the 'funnelling effect'.

And here we can see how far human beings have evolved beyond all other animals. For a chimpanzee, a book or a photograph or a blue film would be as abstract as an algebraic formula. Our right brain obligingly adds a third dimension of reality, so that we are sexually stimulated by an abstraction. We can even *imagine* a sexual stimulus and experience the same response.

All of which demonstrates that we already know the answer. It lies in the deliberate use of 'the funnel'.

Let us look more closely at the mechanics of this process of 'funnelling'. I am relaxed in an armchair. I idly pick up a child's schoolbook that lies on the floor – an anthology of poetry. In a spirit of nostalgia I turn the pages: 'Elegy written in a Country Churchyard', 'The Daffodils', 'Ode to the West Wind', 'Full fathom five'. . . . As I read Gray's 'Elegy', I conjure up a picture of a church-bell, a herd of cows, a tired ploughman. But because I am relaxed, I add other things that Gray forgot to include: the plop of cow dung on the muddy road and its not-unpleasant grassy smell, the moss on the gravestones, the cool smell of the air after a shower. Phrases like 'glimmering landscape', 'drowsy tinklings', 'ivy-mantled tower', 'blazing hearth', all bring a trickle of delight, and encourage my 'other self' to supply more details. When he speaks of swallows twittering in a straw-built shed, my mind supplies the smell of the straw. And when I have finished the poem, I experience a deep inner calm, a sense of relaxation, of relief. It doesn't matter that much of the poem seems old-fashioned, and that it has more than a touch of sermonizing. Gray has demonstrated to me what my mind can do. It can take me out of this armchair, to other times and other places. When I turn to Shelley's 'Ode to the West Wind', my mind creates the roaring of wind in trees and the smell of autumn leaves; when Wordsworth speaks of 'old unhappy far-off things', my mind slips into history, and I realize that even if my own life is limited to three score and ten, I am the only animal who can look back down the corridors of history just as I can look down on the world from an aeroplane.

There can be no doubt whatever: *I* have re-created Gray's country churchyard and Wordsworth's daffodils and Shelley's autumn woods. This 'I' is Howard Miller's 'unit of pure thought'. And it is capable of far more than conjuring up a few mental images: a beach in summer, a mountain landscape. It is perfectly willing to take me on mental voyages. When my child comes and switches on the television set, I realize that these trivial soap operas and situation comedies are based on the false assumption, that our imagination is limited. Having just returned from this mental voyage, I only feel saddened by these crude attempts to engage my attention.

Yet this is hardly the fault of the television companies. For how often do I try to use that power of the mind? When I feel tired, I pick up a newspaper, or look in the TV guide. My leisure is controlled by this assumption that that world 'out there' is *the* reality, and that if I close my eyes, I shall fall asleep.

But let me try to grasp the implications of what has just happened. The old lamp in the woodshed is an Aladdin's lamp, which can release a genie who is willing to take me voyages on a magic carpet. The absurd thing is that I have known about him since childhood; he has been taking me on these voyages ever since my mother read me *Jack and the Beanstalk*. But I have made the false assumption that these voyages were a kind of dream. They also seemed to depend upon some factor that I could not control: so that even with a free evening and a good book, I could still not be sure whether the magic carpet would float off the ground, or leave me sitting there. More often than not, it left me sitting there. So I have come to feel that the carpet is thoroughly unreliable. Now I can see that the fault lay in me. I have simply failed to achieve the correct conditions: to relax, to still the senses, to 'funnel' my mental energies into the book.

Sometimes, there seems to be some obscure dissatisfaction in me that resists the whole process, a kind of tension. If I analyse this more closely, I see that it springs from another misunderstanding. I am inclined to assume that my own role is passive; I sit down with the book, and wait for it to 'transport' me. But if I study the experience of being deeply moved by poetry, I see that *I* have to do half the work. I request my right brain to conjure up the country churchyard. I say, 'How about some cow dung?', 'How about the smell of straw?', 'How about some moonlight reflected on a pond?', and my right brain obliges. They have entered into a state of mutual understanding, of collaboration. It is a process of dialogue. So again, the lesson is: I must establish communication with my genie. It is not his fault if he is ignored and forgotten.

In short, the lesson of the experience is the recognition: 'Now I have a partner.' It is analogous to falling in love and realizing that your feelings are reciprocated. 'I' am not alone. What I now have to do is to recognize the implications of this discovery. To some extent, I have always known them. For example, if I need to wake up at seven in the morning, some inner alarm clock will awaken me at precisely seven. This depends, to some extent, on self-confidence. If I am feeling tense and nervous, I shall probably wake up half a dozen times in the night, and then oversleep. But this is because I believe I am alone. If I am feeling healthy and cheerful, my confidence somehow activates that 'other self', which gives me a good night's sleep and awakens me at the right time. I must come to take the existence of this 'other self' for granted, as a basic, unforgettable fact, I must use it and learn to communicate with it. Once I can accept its existence as an incontrovertible fact, then I can begin to persuade it to cooperate on projects that would once have seemed impossible.

To begin with, it is the answer to the problem Maslow thought insoluble: how to summon 'peak experiences' at will. The technique is for the 'me', the left-brain self, to build up optimism and self-confidence, the certainty that 'all is well'. (And this is the easiest thing in the world; I just did it spontaneously as I wrote the previous sentence.) We can study this simplest of all mechanisms in all moments of contentment – by recalling, for example, what it was like as a child on Christmas Day: that increasing feeling of 'trust', of happy expectancy. When the left brain tells itself, 'All is well,' the right responds with a glow of warmth, a trickle of sheer joy. I am, in effect, re-programming my subconscious, my 'under-floor lightning'.

It is true that if I have been feeling depressed, I may find it difficult to convince myself that 'all is well'; some diminutive sceptic inside me mutters, 'Oh yeah?' Here it is important to grasp Howard Miller's central recognition: that the 'I' is the master of consciousness. The presence of the inner sceptic is unimportant; he will eventually be overruled by majority opinion. Meanwhile, the 'I' must state: 'It is an *objective* fact that all is well.' For this is the very heart of the matter. We are speaking of objectivity. Most human unhappiness is due to subjectivity, our tendency to be dominated by emotions we know to be 'false', yet which seem to cling with the persistency of leeches. We evolve by forcing these emotions to obey the rule of law, of objectivity.

As soon as we induce these states of inner certainty, we begin to observe their effect. We become less 'accident-prone'. Some sixth sense helps to steer us clear of trouble. Interesting coincidences begin to occur. (When I become subject to these synchronicities, I know I am in good health.) We may begin to have flashes of pre-cognition; the telephone rings and you know who it is before you answer it. You know that a letter from a long-lost friend will arrive in the post. In short, the right brain seems to control certain paranormal powers, and is willing to place them at the disposal of the left. The *kahunas* assert that the 'higher self' can control the future; and everyone who has experienced moods of relaxed self-confidence knows that curious inner certainty that nothing is going to go wrong.

The most interesting possibility remains the prospect of unlimited 'access to inner worlds'. The 'natural' view of our inner world is that it consists of feelings, memories, emotions, and that these are necessarily limited. The Proustian 'glimpses' make us aware that this is untrue. The 'library' contains detailed recordings of everything that has ever happened to us, and these can be recombined in any order. Just as a simple knowledge of algebra provides me with the basis for solving *any* algebraic problem, so a fairly small range of experience can provide us with the material for constructing a vast range of 'other realities'. We catch a glimpse of this inventiveness in dreams, or in 'hypnagogic states' (between sleeping and waking); but these are obviously some kind of random selection. Our inner librarian does his best work when we *ask for* his cooperation. When, for example, I am reading a book about Paris in the nineteenth century, he helpfully conjures up a vast range of images, from Balzac, Zola, Maupassant to the Impressionist painters to my own memory of the sights and smells of the Left Bank. He only does this when I am thoroughly relaxed and absorbed; but when he chooses to do it, he evokes a Paris which is actually far richer than any physical experience of the real place.

This ability to 'real-ize' another time and place I call Faculty X. It is quite clearly a natural ability we all possess, but that we fail to understand. The glimpses of the romantics were glimpses of Faculty X; and, as we have seen, they concluded that they come and go as they please. Only now, more than a century later, are we beginning to recognize that such states *are* within our control; not only that, but that they offer the promise of the most fascinating step in human evolution so far. When we study the long course of evolution, from the crude instinctive consciousness of the animal to our own sophisticated and complex self-awareness, it suddenly becomes clear that the main direction of this evolution has been the conscious control of Faculty X.

In *Back to Methuselah*, Shaw suggested that human beings would have to learn to live for at least three centuries in order to begin to realize their possibilities; seventy or eighty years is simply not enough. As to how this would come about, Shaw explained that once human beings had become conscious of the necessity, the rest would follow automatically. The unconscious mind would do the rest. 'The brain shall not fail when the will is in earnest.' At the time, this struck many of Shaw's admirers as the least plausible part of his theory – human beings are used to struggling for what they want. But we can see that it is a plain statement of fact about Faculty X. The crucial step in individual evolution is quite simply to recognize the existence of that 'other self'. When this happens, we are ready to embark upon the most interesting experiment of all: to discover what our two selves can do when they enter into active collaboration.

For myself, I must acknowledge that Brad's description of his experiences brought new levels of insight into this whole problem of 'visionary consciousness' and the two selves. The pressures of writing a quarter of a million words in four months had made me aware that I had to stop treating this as a problem for 'me alone'. I had to assume that something inside me would respond to the urgency and take on half the work. And as I slaved away, I became aware of a sensation that something was happening: rather as if someone had taken hold of the other end of the double-handed saw. There was no possibility of relaxation: I still had to do my part. But there was a comforting sense of having a willing helper. I have always been too inclined to drive myself, too inclined to grit my teeth and rely on sheer force and stubbornness. And I have a deep distrust of anything that looks like self-pity or self-indulgence, for these have been far more responsible than material hardship for the destruction of many 'Outsiders'. But under pressure, this attitude of mind can lead to fatalism and pessimism. As I wrote chapter after chapter of the Rasputin novel, then of *Poltergeist*, the pessimism began to give way to a cautious, realistic optimism.

At Viittakivi, I tried to convey to my students what I felt to be the central lesson of the previous six months: that *we* must be in charge of our own emotions. The logical answer to someone who says, 'I am depressed', is, 'Ok. Un-depress yourself.' To demonstrate the point, I asked the students to meditate upon the most depressing thoughts they could call to mind. Within a few minutes, most of them were looking thoroughly gloomy. Then they were told: 'Now snap out of it.' 'Under orders', they found this fairly easy to do – easier than it might have been if they were alone. On the last day, all the groups met together in the main hall, and various spokesmen tried to explain what they had been doing. The woman who spoke for our group said: 'Mr Wilson taught us how to make ourselves depressed,' and there was a roar of laughter. Yet she *had* stated the essence of those group sessions. If you can raise yourself out of depression by an act of will, then you can also raise yourself out of 'normal consciousness' into the peak experience.

One of my literary chores during the earlier part of the year had been writing an introduction to *The Occult Establishment* by the late James Webb. Webb, one of the most brilliant minds of his generation, had committed suicide the previous year, after a two-year mental illness. In the latter part of his illness, he had kept up a correspondence with Joyce Collin-Smith, which she allowed me to read. It was clear that he had gone through a rather more severe version of my 'panic attacks', complete with delusions and hallucinations. He had allowed himself to be 'taken in' by the depressions and, as a result, had been drawn far deeper into 'negative feedback'. Yet he fought back, and in those final months seemed to be regaining his balance, and recognizing that he had achieved completely new insights into the problems that interested him so deeply – the hidden powers of the mind. The suicide seems to have been due to a momentary regression into pessimism. The Introduction remained unpublished, because his wife disagreed with my view of his illness – she preferred to believe that it was ordinary insanity. But my study of Webb's last letters made me more aware than ever of the nature of this problem. We 'identify' with our emotions. When I have a pain, I say, '*It* hurts.' not, 'I hurt.'

Yet when I experience happiness I say, '*I am* happy;' and when I experience depression, I say, '*I* feel gloomy.' Writing about James Webb made me more convinced that feelings – particularly negative feelings – are an irrelevancy. The 'central ego', the 'unit of pure thought', must learn to recognize that it remains the final arbiter. Feeling, like perception, is intentional.

But these prescriptions seemed negative: to decline to be 'taken in' by feelings, to regard a sudden depression as objectively as you would regard a bruised knee-cap or a cold in the head. These formulae amounted to self-discipline, but the problem was not self-discipline so much as how to enlist the active support of that 'other self'. This was the problem that preoccupied me when I arrived in Finland; this was the problem to which Brad presented me with a simple and unambiguous answer. Brad told me, in effect: 'There is no problem whatever in contacting your "other self". It is perfectly willing to contact you. You merely have to be willing to listen.'

'Listening' must here be understood as an active suspension of our automatic functions, an attitude of vigilance, of alertness. Most of us waste about 90 per cent of our lives in purely automatic living. In order to suspend this, I merely have to behave as if I am listening intently for some important noise, like the ringing of a telephone. And as I remain in this condition of 'openness', my vital powers begin to rise in me, like water in a well.

When I asked Brad to summarize the long-term results of his experience, he replied in a long letter:

'During all these years there has been a continuing diffusion of movement-impulse moments into all possible areas of life – not continuously timewise, but whenever I choose to let it happen. And I have chosen to do so in many different kinds of situations: when teaching, when taking part in a discussion, when in sexual intercourse, when spending a day in town, when taking a shower, when preparing a lesson or talk, very often in the preparation of these materials for you. This "choosing to do so" means making the inner gesture of becoming silent and empty for a brief moment, a letting the decision about "what next" rise to the surface and take form via movement impulses.

'It has taken me several years to realize and learn that although this dimension of experience emerged "by chance" in my life, it will continue only "by choice", i.e. by clear conscious wanting or willing to make the inner gesture of change-over from my usual mind-directed level of conscious behaviour in a situation, to the "movement-impulse level" which I feel represents a more wholly integrated level of response in which my mind is just a part, co-existing and collaborating with many other levels of myself, of my person.'

One area in which Brad feels there has been a decisive change in his life is that of human relationships:

'In recent years, and during this last year more than ever before, some kind of 'living with love" or "living in love" has characterized my living, and it has been transforming my experiences with my students, my fellow teachers, my friends and acquaintances. Earlier in my life, from my teens onward, my tendency was to limit and confine this sort of "whole open being and sharing" to one chosen relationship at a time, and, while that relationship continued, not allow myself to have other "meetings" with others. There was a popular song in the 1940s: "When I'm not near the girl I love, I love the girl I'm near." But because I was living according to a closed-relationship morality, those words were very threatening to me then. Now, I see the possibility of giving a new interpretation to them – of understanding them to mean the deep promise of an open relationship morality. Just this transition from closed exclusive relationships to open inclusive relationships is the direction of my growth and development at present. . . . Because so much of my life has been spent within a closed-relationship framework of values, now my venturing into the territory of open relationships is like moving in a new, unexplored territory without a map or compass. It is both thrilling and threatening.

'Long ago, in an experience, I felt myself almost disintegrating into a flood of fear (my "baby at the bottom of the well" experience). Now I have moments when I'm almost disintegrating into a flood of joy . . . each cell would float off buoyantly in a different direction. . . . Recently, I have been experiencing these "deep peaks" several times a week. It has been like riding waves from crest to crest without touching bottom in between. . . .'

Brad seems to feel that these basic changes may be regarded as a preparation for the second part of his life. 'I expressed this latter feeling last year when I told a friend that I felt that something in me was getting ready to be born, and that I felt as though I were the baby, the mother and the midwife, all at the same time.'

Brad does not regard his present situation as some kind of ultimate. All stages are transitional. Brad seems to me to have made an important discovery about how we can enter into a new relationship with the unknown areas of the mind. Yet his own experience has not been so much one of 'access to inner worlds' as of an active collaboration with that 'other self' in *this* world. He remarks that new possibilities 'will open up as I become stronger and clearer in my ability to will the inner gesture of change-over from my usual mind-directed level of conscious behaviour to the movement-impulse level'. He recognizes that the present stage is as rudimentary as a baby's first efforts to walk or use its hand for grasping. 'Whether the strengthening of my will will lead only to more sustained and continuous periods of living from that level, or whether it will also lead to new levels of experience, I do not know.' Neither is it important that he does not know. All that matters is to know that in our generation, in the last part of the twentieth century, a new direction of evolution has suddenly opened up in front of us.

Index